**Cultural And
Geographical
Exploration**

The
Ancient Incas

CHRONICLES FROM *NATIONAL GEOGRAPHIC*

Cultural And Geographical Exploration

**Cultural And
Geographical
Exploration**

The
Ancient Incas

CHRONICLES FROM *NATIONAL GEOGRAPHIC*

Arthur M. Schlesinger, jr.
Senior Consulting Editor

Fred L. Israel
General Editor

CHELSEA HOUSE PUBLISHERS

Philadelphia

CHELSEA HOUSE PUBLISHERS

Editor in Chief Stephen Reginald
Managing Editor James D. Gallagher
Production Manager Pamela Loos
Art Director Sara Davis
Director of Photography Judy L. Hasday
Senior Production Editor Lisa Chippendale

First Printing

1 3 5 7 9 8 6 4 2

Library of Congress Cataloging-in-Publication Data

Bingham, Hiram, 1875–1956.
    The ancient Incas / Hiram Bingham.
        p.   cm. — (Cultural & geographic exploration)
    Includes bibliographical references and index.
    ISBN 0-7910-5104-8
    1. Machu Picchu site (Peru)—Juvenile literature.   2. Incas—
Antiquities—Juvenile literature.   3. Bingham, Hiram, 1875–1956—
Journeys—Peru—Juvenile literature.   5. Peru—Description and
Travel—Juvenile literature.   I. Title.   II. Series: Cultural and
geographical exploration.
    F3429.1.M3B57   1999
    985ı.37—dc21   98-45472
                                                                                CIP
                                                                                AC

CONTENTS

"THE GREATEST EDUCATIONAL JOURNAL"

When the first *National Geographic* magazine appeared in October 1888, the United States totaled 38 states. Grover Cleveland was President. The nation's population hovered around 60 million. Great Britain's Queen Victoria also ruled as the Empress of India. William II became Kaiser of Germany that year. Tsar Alexander III ruled Russia and the Turkish Empire stretched from the Balkans to the tip of Arabia. To Westerners, the Far East was still a remote and mysterious land. Throughout the world, riding the back of an animal was the principle means of transportation. Unexplored and unmarked places dotted the global map.

On January 13, 1888, thirty-three men—scientists, cartographers, inventors, scholars, and explorers—met in Washington, D. C. They had accepted an invitation from Gardiner Greene Hubbard (1822-1897), the first president of the Bell Telephone Co. and a leader in the education of the deaf, to form the National Geographic Society "to increase and diffuse geographic knowledge." One of the assembled group noted that they were the "first explorers of the Grand Canyon and the Yellowstone, those who had carried the American flag farthest north, who had measured the altitude of our famous mountains, traced the windings of our coasts and rivers, determined the distribution of flora and fauna, enlightened us in the customs of the aborigines, and marked out the path of storm and flood." Nine months later, the first issue of *National Geographic* magazine was sent out to 165 charter members. Today, more than a century later, membership has grown to an astounding 11 million in more than 170 nations. Several times that number regularly read the monthly issues of the *National Geographic* magazine.

The first years were difficult ones for the new magazine. The earliest volumes seem dreadfully scientific and quite dull. The articles in Volume I, No. 1 set the tone—W. M Davis, "Geographic Methods in Geologic Investigation," followed by W. J. McGee, "The Classification of Geographic Forms by Genesis." Issues came out erratically—three in 1889, five in 1890, four in 1891; and two in 1895. In January 1896 "an illustrated monthly" was added to the title. The November issue that year contained a photograph of a half-naked Zulu bride and bridegroom in their wedding finery staring full face into the camera. But, a reader must have wondered what to make of the accompanying text: "These people . . . possess some excellent traits, but are horribly cruel when once they have smelled blood." In hopes of expanding circulation, the Board of Managers offered newsstand copies at $.25 each and began to accept advertising. But the magazine essentially remained unchanged. Circulation only rose slightly.

In January 1898, shortly after Gardiner Greene Hubbard's death, his son-in-law Alexander Graham Bell (1847-1922) agreed to succeed him as the second president of the National Geographic Society. Bell invented the telephone in 1876 and, while pursuing his life long goal of improving the lot of the deaf, had turned his amazingly versatile mind to contemplating such varied problems as human flight, air conditioning, and popularizing geography. The society then had about 1100 members—the magazine was on the edge of bankruptcy. Bell did not want the job. He wrote in his diary though that he accepted leadership of the Society "in order to save it. Geography is a fascinating subject and it can be made interesting," he told the board of directors. Bell abandoned the unsuccessful attempt to increase circulation through newsstand sales. "Our journal," he wrote "should go to members, people who believe in our work and want to help." He understood that the lure for prospective members should be an association with a society that made it possible for the average person to share with kings and scientists the excitement of sending an expedition to a strange land or an explorer to an inaccessible region. This idea, more than any other, has been responsible for the growth of the National Geographic Society and for the popularity of the magazine. "I can well remember," recalled Bell in 1912, "how the idea was laughed at that we should ever reach a membership of ten thousand." That year it had soared to 107,000!

Bell attributed this phenomenal growth though to one man who had transformed the *National Geographic* magazine into "the greatest educational journal in the world"—Gilbert H. Grosvenor (1875-1966). Bell had hired the then 24-year-old Grosvenor in 1899 as the Society's first full-time employee "to put some life into the magazine." He personally escorted the new editor, who will become his son-in-law, to the Society's headquarters—a small rented room shared with the American Forestry Association on the fifth floor of a building, long since gone, across 15th street from the U. S. Treasury in downtown Washington. Grosvenor remembered the headquarters "littered with old magazines, newspapers, and a few record books and six enormous boxes crammed with *Geographics* returned by the newsstands." "No desk!" exclaimed Bell. "I'll send you mine." That afternoon, delivery men brought Grosvenor a large walnut rolltop and the new editor began to implement Bell's instructions—to transform the magazine from one of cold geographic fact "expressed in hieroglyphic terms which the layman could not understand into a vehicle for carrying the living, breathing, human-interest truth about this great world of ours to the people." And what did Bell consider appropriate "geographic subjects?" He replied: "The world and all that is in it is our theme."

Grosvenor shared Bell's vision of a great society and magazine which would disseminate geographic knowledge. "I thought of geography in terms of its Greek root: *geographia*—a description of the world," he later wrote. "It thus becomes the most catholic of subjects, universal in appeal, and embracing nations, people, plants, birds, fish. We would never lack interesting subjects." To attract readers, Grosvenor had to change the public attitude toward geography which he knew was regarded as "one of the dullest of all subjects, something to inflict upon schoolboys and avoid in later life." He wondered why certain books which relied heavily on geographic description remained popular—Charles Darwin's *Voyage of the Beagle*, Richard Dana, Jr.'s *Two Years Before the Mast* and even Herodotus' *History*. Why did readers for generations, and with Herodotus' travels, for twenty centuries return to these books? What did these volumes, which used so many geographic descriptions, have in common? What was the secret? According to Grosvenor, the answer was that "each was an accurate, eyewitness, firsthand account. Each contained simple straightforward writing—writing that sought to make pictures in the reader's mind."

Gilbert Grosvenor was editor of the *National Geographic* magazine for 55 years, from 1899 until 1954. Each of the 660 issues under his direction had been a highly readable geography textbook. He took Bell's vision and made it a reality. Acclaimed as "Mr. Geography," he discovered the earth anew for himself and for millions around the globe. He charted the dynamic course which the National Geographic Society and its magazine followed for more than half a century. In so doing, he forged an instrument for world education and understanding unique in this or any age. Under his direction, the *National Geographic* magazine grew from a few hundred copies—he recalled carrying them to the post office on his back—to more than five million at the time of his retirement as editor, enough for a stack 25 miles high.

This Chelsea House series celebrates Grosvenor's first twenty-five years as editor of the *National Geographic*. "The mind must see before it can believe," said Grosvenor. From the earliest days, he filled the magazine with photographs and established another Geographic principle—to portray people in their natural attire or lack of it. Within his own editorial committee, young Grosvenor encountered the prejudice that photographs had to be "scientific." Too often, this meant dullness. To Grosvenor, every picture and sentence had to be interesting to the layman. "How could you educate and inform if you lost your audience by boring your readers?" Grosvenor would ask his staff. He persisted and succeeded in making the *National Geographic* magazine reflect this fascinating world.

To the young-in-heart of every age there is magic in the name *National Geographic*. The very words conjure up enchanting images of faraway places, explorers and scientists, sparkling seas and dazzling mountain peaks, strange plants, animals, people, and customs. The small society founded in 1888 "for the increase and diffusion of geographic knowledge" grew, under the guidance of one man, to become a great force for knowledge and understanding. This achievement lies in the genius of Gilbert H. Grosvenor, the architect and master builder of the National Geographic Society and its magazine.

Fred L. Israel
The City College of the City University of New York

HIRAM BINGHAM AND MACHU PICCHU

FRED L. ISRAEL

Hiram Bingham's 1906–11 explorations in South America were so important that when he sought funds for another Peruvian expedition in 1912, the National Geographic Society gave him a grant which was matched by Yale University. Bingham's work is one of the most remarkable shows of archaeological exploration in South America. He publicized the thrilling wonders and mysteries of the nearly inaccessible city of Machu Picchu. What extraordinary people the builders of Machu Picchu must have been to have constructed, without steel and using hammers and wedges, this wonderful city on a mountain top.

Hiram Bingham (1875–1956) was born in Honolulu, the son and grandson of missionaries. His paternal grandfather, Hiram, was among the first Christian missionaries to reach the Hawaiian Islands (1820) and is responsible for translating the New Testament into Hawaiian (1825–39). His son, also Hiram, translated the New Testament into the language of Gilbertese (1857–1873), peculiar to the Gilbert Islands which lie along the Pacific equator.

Hiram Bingham graduated from Yale in 1898. He, too, prepared for a missionary career but found himself "unhappy" with the work. While in Hawaii, he met and married Alfreda Mitchell, the granddaughter of Charles L. Tiffany, founder of Tiffany and Company. They had seven sons.

Bingham received an M.A. from the University of California (1900), followed during the next five years by another M.A. and a Ph.D. in the then relatively little-studied field of South American history. In 1906, restless and ambitious, Bingham retraced the 1890 path of Bolivar across the northern coast of South America in preparation for a biography. This difficult and dangerous route from Caracas to Bogota was described in Bingham's first work, *The Journal of an Expedition Across Venezuela and Columbia* (1909). Upon his return in 1907, Bingham took a position as lecturer in South American history and geography at Yale. He became an assistant professor of Latin American history in 1910 and was professor from 1915–24.

Teaching did not stop Bingham's urge to explore. In 1909, he undertook a six-month trek retracing the old Spanish colonial trade route from Buenos Aires through the Andes to Lima. He described his adventure in *Across South America* (1911).

In 1911, Bingham directed the Yale Peruvian Expedition to search for Machu Picchu, the lost city of the Incas—the Inca dynasty had reigned from ca. 1200 A.D.–1572 A.D. Prospects for locating it were poor; not even the Spanish conquistadores had discovered it. The jungle had engulfed the remains of the Inca civilization. Roots of towering trees had pried open the temples. Centuries passed. It was believed that Machu Picchu was situated near Cuzco, Peru. Clues from Inca chronicles were scant. The expedition owed its success to Bingham's steadfastness.

On July 24, 1911, Bingham reached Machu Picchu. Perched between two sharp peaks, the city had managed to escaped detection by the Spaniards. Machu Picchu is one of the few pre-Columbian urban centers found nearly intact. The site, about five square miles in area, includes a temple, similar to the Temple of the Sun at Cuzco, and a citadel—both surrounded by terraced gardens linked by more than 3000 steps. The 1912 expedition excavated the site.

The magnificent ruins of Machu Picchu are the most spectacular source for understanding Inca civilization. "The sight held me spellbound," wrote Bingham. "Would anyone believe what I have found?" Now daily jets fly tourists of many nationalities to Cuzco and hundreds each day make the trip to Machu Picchu. But what was this city? Conjectures range widely: birthplace of the Inca Empire; a military outpost in the mountains; an imperial retreat; a ceremonial center? The National Geographic Society and Yale University sponsored his expedition in 1912 and 1914–15. Bingham's discoveries in Peru became the basis for a series of lectures and books including *Inca Land* (1922); *Machu Picchu: Citadel of the Incas* (1930); and *Lost City of the Incas* (1948, 1965).

In the 1920s, Bingham began another career, in Republican party politics—serving Connecticut as Lieutenant Governor (1923–25); Governor (1925); and Senator (1925–33). In 1951, President Truman asked Bingham to head the Loyalty Review Board of the Civil Service Commission (1951–53).

VOL. XXIV, No. 4　　　　WASHINGTON　　　　APRIL, 1913

IN THE WONDERLAND OF PERU

THE WORK ACCOMPLISHED BY THE PERUVIAN EXPEDITION OF 1912, UNDER THE AUSPICES OF YALE UNIVERSITY AND THE NATIONAL GEOGRAPHIC SOCIETY

BY HIRAM BINGHAM, DIRECTOR OF THE EXPEDITION

Prof. Hiram Bingham's explorations in South America, 1906–1911, and particularly his discoveries in 1911, were so important that when he was seeking funds for another Peruvian expedition in 1912, the Research Committee of the National Geographic Society made him a grant of $10,000, Yale University contributing an equal amount. His preliminary report to the National Geographic Society and Yale University of the work done in 1912 is printed herewith, and forms one of the most remarkable stories of exploration in South America in the past 50 years. The members of the Society are extremely gratified at the splendid record which Dr. Bingham and all the members of the expedition have made, and as we study the marvelous pictures which are printed with this report, we also are thrilled by the wonders and mystery of Machu Picchu. What an extraordinary people the builders of Machu Picchu must have been to have constructed, without steel implements, and using only stone hammers and wedges, the wonderful city of refuge on the mountain top.—EDITOR.

INTRODUCTORY

THE Peruvian Expedition of 1912, under the auspices of Yale University and the National Geographic Society, was organized with the specific purpose of carrying on the work begun by the Yale Peruvian Expedition of 1911. It was not intended to cover such a large area as had been done the year before, but to do intensive work in a part of the field where only reconnaissance work had been previously attempted.

The staff of the expedition consisted of the following: Prof. Hiram Bingham, director; Prof. Herbert E. Gregory, geologist; Dr. George F. Eaton, osteologist; Mr. Albert H. Bumstead,

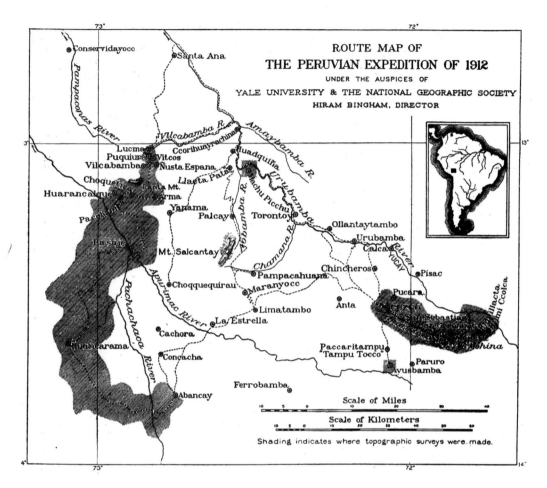

ROUTE MAP OF
THE PERUVIAN EXPEDITION OF 1912
UNDER THE AUSPICES OF
YALE UNIVERSITY & THE NATIONAL GEOGRAPHIC SOCIETY
HIRAM BINGHAM, DIRECTOR

Scale of Miles

Scale of Kilometers

Shading indicates where topographic surveys were made.

MAP OF REGION EXPLORED BY YALE–NATIONAL GEOGRAPHIC SOCIETY EXPEDITION

The dotted lines indicate the routes taken by various members of the expedition and show how thoroughly the country was covered during 1912. The shaded areas indicate the extent of the careful topographical surveys. The black spot on the little map of South America in the corner indicates the location and extent of the route map.

chief topographer; Mr. Ellwood C. Erdis, archeological engineer; Dr. Luther T. Nelson, surgeon; Messrs. Kenneth C. Heald and Robert Stephenson, assistant topographers, and Messrs. Paul Bestor, Osgood Hardy, and Joseph Little, assistants.

The director, osteologist, and the two assistant topographers left New York May 16, and were followed three weeks later by most of the others. The geologist was not able to leave until August: but as the plans for his work called for a study of a comparatively small region, the

Photo by Hiram Bingham

STRAW BOATS ON THE BEACH AT PACASMAYO, PERU

On their way to southern Peru the members of the expedition touched at various ports, including Pacasmayo, where the fishermen use a peculiar form of canoe. These canoes, or *balsas*, are made of rushes and have to be dried out each time they are used. The picture also shows a typical fisherman's hut made of split bamboo.

three months that he was able to spend in Peru were sufficient for his needs. Practically the entire party returned to New York in the latter part of December, after an absence of seven months.

With one exception, the members of the expedition enjoyed fairly good health during their stay in the field. An occasional acute gastritis or enteritis resulted from indiscretions in diet. Assistant Hardy and the soldier who accompanied the topographical party suffered a slight attack of malaria, but this was soon overcome by quinine.

In making a reconnaissance of the extremely inaccessible and primitive ruins on the mountain of Huayna Picchu, Assistant Topographer Heald was so unfortunate as to lose his foothold on the verge of a precipice, and had a very narrow escape from death. This accident resulted in a rupture of the ligaments of his collar-bone, which later incapacitated him for some time and prevented his accomplishing the reconnaissance work in the Pampaconas Valley which had been planned.

Assistant Bestor had the misfortune to contract amœbic dysentery while on a journey in the interior. Very probably he was infected by drinking unboiled water from the Apurimac River at Pasaje. His condition failed to improve after seven weeks of treatment, and he was obliged to return to the United States. He was kindly received at Ancon Hospital, and was there put on the road to complete recovery.

We found an epidemic of smallpox and typhoid fever raging in the towns of Arma, Pu-quiura, and Lucma. These towns of 150 to 200 inhabitants had had a death toll of 40 and 50 people each.

There was very little opportunity for medical work among the native Indians, but the more educated Peruvians were extremely glad to come to the free clinics.

There are no physicians in most of the villages of the interior; consequently the owners of the large plantations have to rely entirely on their own efforts at curing diseases among the Indians in their employ. Very few Peruvians are properly vaccinated.

Photo by Hiram Bingham

IN FRONT OF THE CATHEDRAL: LIMA, PERU

The first part of the expedition arrived in Lima just in time to witness the annual procession of Corpus Christi. Starting from the cathedral, shown at the right, the procession, made up largely of little children in attractive costumes, passed around the four sides of the principal plaza and returned to the cathedral. This picture, taken before the procession started, shows the military band and escort, and the carpet of flowers and green leaves over which the procession was to pass.

Photo by Hiram Bingham

CORPUS CHRISTI PROCESSION: LIMA, PERU

After Benediction had been given on the corner of the plaza, the procession moved slowly toward the cathedral. The "conflict of old and new" is vividly emphasized in this picture, where the repair wagon of the trolley line is seen at the right only a few feet from this religious procession so redolent of the middle ages. The towers of the cathedral are made of plaster and lath. In this land of earthquakes it was not considered safe to build them of stone.

ALPACAS AND LLAMAS

On the high upland pastures between Lake Titicaca and Cuzco thousands of alpacas and llamas find their natural feeding grounds. They have been domesticated for centuries, and do not exist in a wild state, but are always attended by shepherds. Alpaca wool is one of the choicest exports of Peru.

A TYPICAL PERUVIAN PLAZA

The llamas are loaded with rock-salt. The open sewer in the center of the street is characteristic of many mountain towns

6

Photo by L. T. Nelson

A GROUP OF INDIAN ALCALDES: SOUTHERN PERU

Near Checcacupe Station was a group of Indian Alcaldes bearing their staffs of office decorated with bands of silver. The Alcalde is the native Indian official who stands between the local government magistrate and the natives of his village, or of his section of a city. They do no manual labor, but frequently have anything but an easy time.

Photo by L. T. Nelson

A SCENE AT SICUANI STATION, SOUTHERN PERU

At the railway stations between Lake Titicaca and Cuzco there were invariably groups of picturesquely clad Indians nearly always wearing a poncho, and sometimes felt hats, but more often the gaudily decorated reversible pancake-hat characteristic of this part of Peru.

STRANGE MODE OF VACCINATION

The Indians believe that vaccination with pus from the lesions of a patient who has died with smallpox confers immunity from the disease. They practice this sort of vaccination, with the result that many who are thus inoculated die from the disease.

There is no attempt made to isolate the smallpox or typhoid patients. Neighbors mingle freely in the huts where the diseases exist, and at the funeral of the dead they have feasts in which every one partakes, many using common cups and dishes. The clothes of the dead are washed in the same stream from which the people in the villages get their drinking water.

There are no windows in the highland huts, and there is no attempt at cleanliness in the dark interiors. Of course, fumigation is unknown and vermin abound.

On many of the large plantations conditions are better. There the owners of the estates vaccinate their Indian tenants and laborers. In some of the villages a priest will vaccinate a few during his annual or semiannual visit, so that some do get the benefit of protection from smallpox. In the cities, on the other hand, while many are vaccinated, there are many who are not, so that even in Cuzco smallpox was raging during our stay; and, furthermore, practically no attempt was being made at isolation or any other measure to prevent the spread of the epidemic.

Notwithstanding many hardships and the presence of a considerable amount of illness in southern Peru, all the members of our party worked hard and faithfully, and the general results of the expedition were highly satisfactory.

RESULTS ACHIEVED BY THE EXPEDITION

The work actually accomplished may be grouped under the following heads: (1) Machu Picchu; its archeology and osteology, and the topography and forestration of the surrounding region.

(2) The Cuzco region; its geology, osteology, and topography, with special reference to the age of its vertebrate remains.

(3) A contour map from Abancay to Puquiura, completing the topography of the cross-section from Camaná, on the Pacific Ocean, to canoe navigation on the Urubamba, begun in 1911.

(4) The topography and archeology of Vitcos and vicinity.

Photo by Hiram Bingham

GROUP OF MOUNTAIN INDIANS: SOUTHERN PERU

The Mountain Indians were always interested in our work and usually were content to silently watch the passage of our caravans, or quietly speculate on the activities of the topographical engineer. Once, however, the chief topographer was attacked by a dozen excited Indians who thought that he and his assistant were working some devilment with their strange instruments. Fortunately by diplomatic means they were dissuaded from doing any harm. Note the bare feet of the women at this great altitude, which is over 14,000 feet.

(5) The identification of ancient Inca place names of Vilcabamba that occur in the Spanish chronicles, but do not appear on any known maps.

(6) An archeological and topographical reconnaissance of the hitherto-unexplored Aobamba Valley.

(7) A reconnaissance of the northern route to Choqquequirau and a brief osteological and archeological reconnaissance of that city.

(8) An anthropological study of the highland Indians of southern Peru, including the careful anthropometric measurement of 145 individuals.

(9) The taking of weather observations on the road and in the camps and the establishment at widely different elevations of four meteorological stations along the 71st meridian west of Greenwich.

(10) The collection, wherever practicable, of paleontological, osteological ethnological, and archeological material.

The following report takes up these subjects in the order named.

Photo by L. T. Nelson

A TYPICAL PERUVIAN INDIAN WOMAN AT QUIQUIJANA, SOUTHERN PERU

Indian women in Peru are never idle. Even when walking along the roads they are almost always engaged in spinning with old-fashioned whirl-bobs and spindles such as their ancestors used over a thousand years ago.

CROSSING THE APURIMAC RIVER   Photo by Hiram Bingham

Among the many hardships encountered by the expedition was the difficulty of fording the rivers under adverse circumstances. In this case, at Pasaje on the Apurimac, there was no wood in the immediate vicinity available for rafts, and it was necessary to wait several hours before the local ferryman, who lived more than a mile away on the wrong side of the river, could be aroused by firing of shots to bring his ancient raft to our assistance.

I.
THE CITY OF MACHU PICCHU, THE CRADLE OF THE INCA EMPIRE

In 1911, while engaged in a search for Vitcos, the last Inca capital, I went down the Urubamba Valley asking for reports as to the whereabouts of ruins.

The first day out from Cuzco saw us in Urubamba, the capital of a province, a modern town charmingly located a few miles below Yucay, which was famous for being the most highly prized winter resort of the Cuzco Incas. The next day brought us to Ollantay-tambo, vividly described by Squier in his interesting book on Peru. Its ancient fortress, perched on a rocky eminence that commands a magnificent view up and down the valley, is still one of the most attractive ancient monuments in America.

Continuing on down the valley over a newly constructed government trail, we found ourselves in a wonderful cañon. So lofty are the peaks on either side that although the trail was frequently shadowed by dense tropical jungle, many of the mountains were capped with snow, and some of them had glaciers. There is no val-

Photo by Hiram Bingham

BIRD'S-EYE VIEW OF MACHU PICCHU (DURING CLEARING) AND THE URUBAMBA CAÑON

On top of the ridge at the foot of the hill called Huayna Picchu and protected on all sides by precipices and on three sides by the rapids of the Urubamba River, the wonderful Inca city of Machu Picchu, discovered in 1911, was one of the principal scenes of action of the Peruvian Expedition of 1912. The mountains in the distance forming the fringe of the Grand Cañon of the Urubamba are from five to seven thousand feet above the river, which at this point is six thousand feet above the sea.

ley in South America that has such varied beauties and so many charms.

Not only has it snow-capped peaks, great granite precipices, some of them 2,000 feet sheer, and a dense tropical jungle; it has also many reminders of the architectural achievements of a bygone race. The roaring rapids of the Urubamba are frequently narrowed by skillfully constructed ancient retaining walls. Wherever the encroaching precipices permitted it, the land between them and the river was terraced. With painstaking care the ancient inhabitants rescued every available strip of arable land from the river. On one slightly bend in the river, where there is a particularly good view, and near a foaming waterfall, some ancient chief built a temple whose walls, still standing, only serve to tantalize the traveler, for there is no bridge within two days' journey and the intervening rapids are impassable. On a precipitous and well-nigh impregnable cliff, walls made of stones carefully fitted together had been placed in the weak spots, so that the defenders of the valley, standing on the top of the cliff, might shower rocks on an attacking force without any danger of their enemies being able to scale the cliff.

The road, following in large part an ancient footpath, is sometimes cut out of the side of sheer precipices, and at others is obliged to run on frail brackets propped against the side of overhanging cliffs. It has been an expensive one to build and will be expensive to maintain. The lack of it prevented earlier explorers from penetrating this cañon. Its existence gave us the chance of discovering Machu Picchu.

On the sixth day out from Cuzco we arrived at a little plantation called Mandorpampa. We camped a few rods away from the owner's grass-thatched hut, and it was not long before he came to visit us and to inquire our business. He turned out to be an Indian rather better than the average, but overfond of "fire-water." His occupation consisted in selling grass and pasturage to passing travelers and in occasionally providing them with ardent spirits. He said that on top of the magnificent precipices near by there were some ruins at a place called Machu Picchu, and that there were others still more inaccessible at Huayna Picchu, on a peak not far distant from our camp. He offered to show me the ruins, which he had once visited, if I would pay him well for his services. His idea of proper payment was 50 cents for his day's labor. This did not seem unreasonable, although it was two and one-half times his usual day's wage.

Leaving camp soon after breakfast I joined the guide, and, accompanied by a soldier that had been kindly loaned me by the Peruvian government, plunged through the jungle to the river bank, and came to a shaky little bridge made of four tree trunks bound together with vines and stretching across a stream only a few inches above the roaring rapids. On the other side we had a hard climb; first through the jungle and later up a very stiff, almost precipitous, slope. About noon we reached a little grass hut, where a good-natured Indian family who had been living here for three or four years gave us welcome and set before us gourds full of cool, delicious water and a few cold boiled sweet potatoes.

Apart from another hut in the vicinity and a few stone-faced terraces, there seemed to be little in the way of ruins, and I began to think that my time had been wasted. However, the view was magnificent, the water was delicious, and the shade of the hut most agreeable. So we rested a while and then went on to the top of the ridge. On all sides of us rose the magnificent peaks of the Urubamba Cañon, while 2,000 feet below us the rushing waters of the noisy river, making a great turn, defended three sides of the ridge, on top of which we were hunting for ruins. On the west side of the ridge the three Indian families who had chosen this eagle's nest for their home had built a little path, part of which consisted of crude ladders of vines and tree trunks tied to the face of the precipice.

Presently we found ourselves in the midst of a tropical forest, beneath the shade of whose trees we could make out a maze of ancient walls, the ruins of buildings made of blocks of granite, some of which were beautifully fitted together in the most refined style of Inca architecture. A few rods farther along we came to a little open space, on which were two splendid temples or palaces. The superior character of the stone work, the presence of these splendid edifices, and of what appeared to be an unusually large number of finely constructed stone dwellings, led me to believe that Machu Picchu might prove to be the largest and most important ruin discovered in South America since the days of the Spanish conquest.

A BIT OF THE ROAD NEAR MACHU PICCHU: URUBAMBA RIVER

The surroundings of Machu Picchu are remarkably wild and the scenery is inexpressibly beautiful. The city lies above the precipices which show in the distance in this picture. The road in the foreground was constructed a few years ago at great expense by the Peruvian government. Early explorers, being obliged to avoid this portion of the Urubamba Valley by the absence of any road, were unaware of the whereabouts of Machu Picchu, although rumors of its existence had reached the ears of a French explorer forty years ago.

THE URUBAMBA CAÑON

Photo by Hiram Bingham

A part of the Urubamba Cañon as seen from the top of Machu Picchu Mountain, 4,000 feet above the river.

THE TEMPLE OF THE THREE WINDOWS: MACHU PICCHU

It was this extraordinary temple, whose most characteristic feature is three large windows, a unique occurrence in early Peruvian architecture, that led us to the belief that Machu Picchu might be Tampu Tocco, the mythical place from which the Incas came when they started out to found that great empire which eventually embraced a large part of South America.

THE SACRED PLAZA: MACHU PICCHU

The presence at Machu Picchu of these splendid temples and palaces, the superior character of the stone work, and the unusually large number of finely constructed stone dwellings, inclines us to believe that Machu Picchu is the largest and most important ruin discovered in South America since the days of the Spanish conquest. This picture shows the Sacred Plaza, the Temple of the Three Windows (behind the man), and, at the left, the Chief Temple, the most imposing structure in the city.

16

Photo by Hiram Bingham

YUCAY, THE LOVELIEST SPOT IN SOUTHERN PERU

The beautiful valley of Yucay was that portion of the Urubamba Valley most favored by the Incas of Cuzco for their country houses. This view is unsurpassed for beauty or grandeur by any in Peru, and by few in the world. There is every gradation of color and depth of shadow from the dense blue of the tropical sky past the glittering crests of the glacier-clad Andes down to the exquisite green terraces of the famous gardens of Yucay. Although the bottom of the valley is 9,000 feet above the sea, it enjoys a climate not unlike that of the south of France. The Incas, ever appreciative of beautiful views, built some of their country houses on the most sightly points of this wonderful valley.

A few weeks later I asked Mr. H. L. Tucker, the engineer of the 1911 Expedition, and Mr. Paul Baxter Lanius, the assistant, to go to Machu Picchu and spend three weeks there in an effort to partially clear the ruins and make such a map as was possible in the time at their disposal. The result of this work confirmed me in my belief that here lay a unique opportunity for extensive clearing and excavating.

The fact that one of the most important buildings was marked by three large windows, a rare feature in Peruvian architecture, and that many of the other buildings had windows, added to the significant circumstance that the city was located in the most inaccessible part of the Andes, inclined me to feel that there was a chance that Machu Picchu might prove to be Tampu Tocco, that mythical place from which the Incas had come when they started out to found Cuzco and to make the beginnings of that great empire which was to embrace a large part of South America.

AN ANCIENT INCA TRADITION

A story told to some of the early Spanish chroniclers in regard to that distant historical event runs somewhat as follows:

Thousands of years ago there lived in the highlands of Peru a megalithic folk who developed a remarkable civilization and who left, as architectural records, such cyclopean structures as the fortresses of Sacsahuaman and Ollantaytambo. These people were attacked by barbarian hordes coming from the south—possibly from the Argentine pampas. They were defeated, and fled into one of the most inaccessible Andine cañons. Here, in a region strongly defended by nature, they established themselves; here their descendants lived for several centuries. The chief place was called Tampu Tocco. Eventually regaining their military strength and becoming crowded in this mountainous valley, they left Tampu Tocco, and, under the leadership of three brothers, went out of three windows (or caves) and started for Cuzco.*

The migration was slow and deliberate. They eventually reached Cuzco, and there established the Inca kingdom, which through several centuries spread by conquest over the entire plateau, and even as far south as Chile and as far north as Ecuador.

This Inca empire had reached its height when the Spaniards came. The Spaniards were

* See Markham's "Incas of Peru," Chapter IV.

Photo by H. L. Tucker

THE ANCIENT TERRACES AT PISAC

At the upper end of the Yucay Valley are the ruins of a wonderful Inca temple, or citadel, called Pisac. One of the best descriptions of this well known and important place is in Squier's "Peru," Chapter XXV.

told that Tampu Tocco was at a place called Pacaritampu, a small village a day's journey southwest of Cuzco and in the Apurimac Valley. The chroniclers duly noted this location, and it has been taken for granted ever since that Tampu Tocco was at Pacaritampu.

THE SIGNIFICANCE OF "WINDOWS"

Tampu means "tavern," or "a place of temporary abode." Tocco means "window." The legend is distinctly connected with a place of windows, preferably of three windows, from which the three brothers, the heads of three tribes or clans, started out on the campaign that founded the Inca empire.

So far as I could discover, few travelers have ever taken the trouble to visit Pacaritampu, and no one knew whether there were any buildings with windows, or caves, there.

It was part of our plan to settle this question, and Dr. Eaton undertook the reconnaissance of Pacaritampu. He reports the presence of a small ruin, evidently a kind of rest-house or tavern, pleasantly located in the Apurimac Valley, but not naturally defended by nature and not distinguished by windows. In fact, there are neither windows nor caves in the vicinity, and the general topography does not lend itself to a rational connection with the tradition regarding Tampu Tocco.

THE RUINS OF PISAC

Photo by H. L. Tucker

A nearer view of part of these remarkable ruins, which resemble in the care and exquisite finish of the stone-cutting the best ruins at Machu Picchu and in Cuzco

A BIT OF OLLANTAYTAMBO, SOUTHERN PERU Photo by Hiram Bingham

On top of the crag, which overlooks the little village of Ollantaytambo, the Incas and their predecessors built a remarkable fortress. Some of the single stones used in the construction of this fortress weigh over eight tons.

THE RUINS OF MAUCALLACTA, NEAR PACARITAMPU Photo by G. F. Eaton

A small ruin pleasantly located in the Apurimac Valley. This is the principal ruin of the little group which the Incas made the Spaniards believe was the home of their ancestors. The surrounding country is not naturally defended and the ruins are not distinguished by windows. In other words, this ruin does not fit in with the traditions as described in the text.

The presence at Machu Picchu of three large windows in one of the most conspicuous and best-built structures led me to wonder whether it might not be possible that the Incas had purposely deceived the Spaniards in placing Tampu Tocco southwest of Cuzco when it was actually north of Cuzco, at Machu Picchu.

The Incas knew that Machu Picchu, in the most inaccessible part of the Andes, was so safely hidden in tropical jungles on top of gigantic precipices that the Spaniards would not be able to find it unless they were guided to the spot. It was naturally to their advantage to conceal the secret of the actual location of Tampu Tocco, a place which their traditions must have led them to venerate. The topography of the region meets the necessities of the tradition: The presence of windows in the houses might readily give the name Tampu Tocco, or "place of temporary residence where there are windows," to this place, and the three conspicuous windows in the principal temple fits in well with the tradition of the three brothers coming out of three windows.

The interest in this historical problem, connected with the fact that at Machu Picchu we had a wonderfully picturesque and remarkably large well-preserved city, untouched by Spanish hands, led us to feel that the entire place needed to be cleared of its jungle and carefully studied architecturally and topographically.

Photo by Hiram Bingham

WONDERFUL MASONRY AT MACHU PICCHU

Two of the windows in the remarkable three windowed temple at Machu Picchu, which furnishes part of the convincing evidence that Machu Picchu and not Pacaritampu was the home of the ancestors of the Incas.

A PICTURESQUE PART OF THE GRAND CAÑON OF THE URUBAMBA ON THE ROAD TO
MACHU PICCHU, SOUTHERN PERU

Photo by Hiram Bingham

THE ROAD IN THE URUBAMBA CAÑON NEAR MACHU PICCHU

If it had not been for this new government road cut at great expense in the face of the precipices of the Urubamba Cañon, it would not have been possible for us to have reached the vicinity of Machu Picchu with our mules and supplies. This ancient city is in the heart of a region most wonderfully defended by nature; the most inaccessible part of the Andes.

PART OF THE SACRED PLAZA: MACHU PICCHU

Photo by Hiram Bingham

One of the gable ends of the three-windowed temple. Notice the tremendous size of the granite blocks in the lower part of the wall. The small ventilating window, of which there is one in each end of the building, is not visible when the structure is looked at from below, and does not affect the striking character of the three large windows in the east wall of this building.

DIFFICULTIES OF THE APPROACH TO MACHU PICCHU

We decided to make a thorough hunt for places of burial and to collect as much osteological and ethnological material as could be found. Our task was not an easy one.

The engineers of the 1911 expedition—H. L. Tucker and P. B. Lanius—who had spent three weeks here making a preliminary map, had been unable to use the trail by which I had first visited Machu Picchu, and reported that the trail which they used was so bad as to make it impossible to carry heavy loads over it.

We knew that mule transportation was absolutely impracticable under these conditions,

and that it was simply a question of making a foot-path over which Indian bearers could carry reasonably good-sized packs.

The first problem was the construction of a bridge over the Urubamba River to reach the foot of the easier of the two possible trails.

The little foot-bridge of four logs that I had used when visiting Machu Picchu for the first time, in July, 1911, was so badly treated by the early floods of the rainy season that when Mr. Tucker went to Machu Picchu at my request, two months later, to make the reconnaissance map, he found only one log left, and was obliged to use a difficult and more dangerous trail on the other side of the ridge.

Knowing that probably even this log had gone with the later floods, it was with some apprehension that I started Assistant Topographer Heald out from Cuzco early in July, 1912, with instructions to construct a bridge across the Urubamba River opposite Machu Picchu, and make a good trail from the river to the ruins—a trail sufficiently good for Indian bearers to use in carrying our 60-pound food-boxes up to the camp and later, our 90-pound boxes of potsherds and specimens down to the mule trail near the river.

SOME RAPID BRIDGE BUILDING

At the most feasible point for building a foot-bridge the Urubamba is some 80 feet wide. The roaring rapids are divided into four streams by large boulders in the river at this point. The first reach is 8 feet long, the next nearly 40 feet, the next about 22 feet, and the final one 15 feet.

For material in the construction of the bridge Mr. Heald had hardwood timber growing on the bank of the stream; for tools he had axes, machetes, and picks—all made in Hartford—and a coil of manila rope. For workmen he had 10 unwilling Indians, who had been forced to accompany him by the governor of the nearest town. For "guide, counselor, and friend" he had an excellent Peruvian soldier, who could be counted on to see to it that the Indians kept faithfully at their task. In describing his work, Mr. Heald says:

"The first step was the felling of the timber for the first two reaches. That was

Photo by Hiram Bingham

HEALD'S BRIDGE: MACHU PICCHU

The completed bridge over the rapids of the Urubamba, showing the forked upright still in place. The great difficulty in building this bridge lay in the fact that the timber was of such density that it would not float.

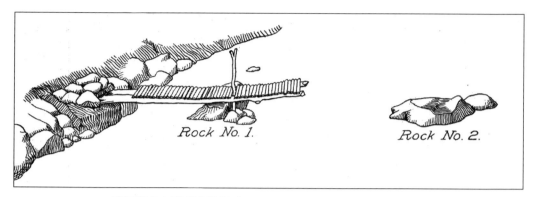

FIGURE 1. THE FIRST STAGE IN MAKING THE BRIDGE
BY WHICH WE CROSSED THE URUBAMBA RIVER
TO REACH THE FOOT OF THE PRECIPICE NEAR MACHU PICCHU

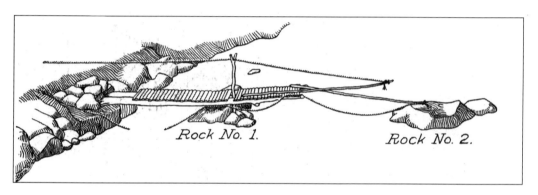

FIGURE 2. "A LONG STRINGER WAS NOW PUSHED OUT ON THE COMPLETED PART
AND THE END THRUST OUT OVER THE WATER"

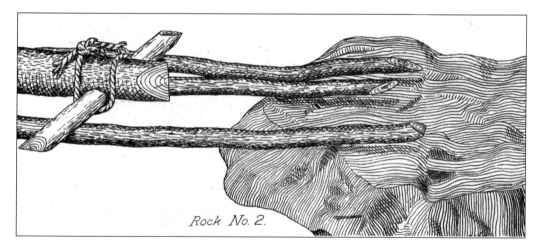

FIGURE 3. THE FINAL STAGE IN GETTING THE HEAVY TIMBER ACROSS THE RAPIDS

quickly done and the short 8-foot space put in place. Then came the task of getting a stringer to the rock forming the next pier. My first scheme was to lay a log in the water, parallel to the bank and upstream from the bridge, and, fastening the lower end, to let the current swing the upper end around until it lodged on the central boulder. On trying this the timber proved to be so heavy that it sank and was lost.

"We next tried building out over the water as far as we could. Two heavy logs were put in place, with their butts on the shore and their outer ends projecting some 10 feet beyond the first span. The shore ends were weighted with rocks and cross-pieces were lashed on with lianas (sinewy vines), making the bridge about 4½ feet wide, as far as it went. Then a forked upright 10 feet high was lashed and wedged into place at the end of the first pier.

THE CROSSING ACHIEVED

"A long, light stringer was now pushed out on the completed part and the end thrust out over the water toward rock No. 2, the end being held up by a rope fastened around it and passing through the fork of the upright.

"This method proved successful, the timber's end being laid on the rock which formed our second pier. Two more light timbers were put across this way, and then a heavy one was tried, part of its weight being borne by the pieces already across by means of a yoke locked in the end. This and another piece were successfully passed over, and after that there was little trouble, cross-pieces being used to form the next and shorter span. . . .

"On the second day of work we finished the bridge about noon and started making a trail up the hill under the guidance of a half-breed who lived in the vicinity. After the first quarter mile

Photo by Hiram Bingham

MACHU PICCHU AND THE WONDERFUL URUBAMBA CAÑON

A general view of the east side of Machu Picchu before the clearing of 1912. One of the most serious difficulties in clearing the ruins was the disposal of the great hardwood trees without destroying the walls of the houses. Huayna Picchu, the ascent of which nearly cost the life of Assistant Topographer Heald, is the peak on the extreme left.

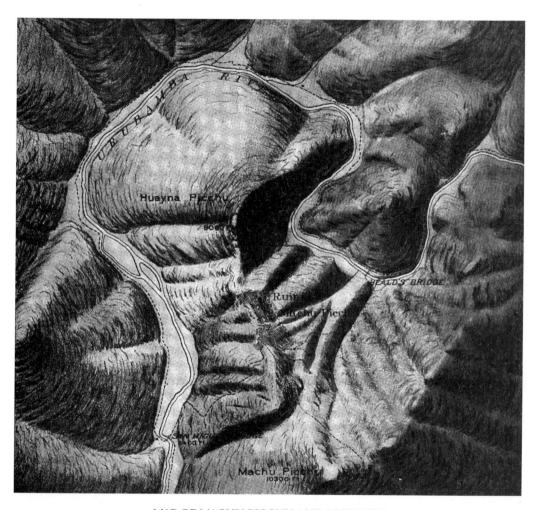

MAP OF MACHU PICCHU AND VICINITY

This relief map of Machu Picchu and vicinity gives a good general idea of the relative position of Heald's bridge, the ruins, and the two peaks—Machu Picchu and Huayna Picchu. It also shows the location of the two trails up from the Urubamba River and enables one to form some conception of the extent of the ruins. The map is misleading in that the precipices are flattened out as they would be if one were looking down upon them from a balloon.

the going was very slow. Not only did the steepness of the slope and the tangled condition of the cane jungle retard us, but the men were very much afraid of snakes, a fear which proved itself

justified, for one of them was very nearly bitten by a little gray snake about 12 inches long.

"The second day's work on the trail took us to the city. The path was still far from being

Photo by Hiram Bingham

Photo by Hiram Bingham

THE BEST TYPE OF INDIAN WORKMAN:
SOUTHERN PERU

Portrait of Enrique Porres, one of the most intelligent workmen that we had to assist in excavating Machu Picchu. In his cheek may be observed a swelling, showing the presence of a quid of coca, the leaves of the plant from which cocaine is extracted. Nearly all the Mountain Indians chew the coca leaf. A quid is carefully made up at the beginning of the day's work, during the middle of the morning, at the commencement of the afternoon's work, and in the middle of the afternoon.

A CHEERFUL WORKMAN FROM CUZCO

Portrait of Alegria, "Mr. Happiness," one of our workmen, who came with us from Cuzco and staid for nearly two months. Most of the workmen were content with what wages they could earn in two weeks, and kept us continually busy trying to replace them.

finished, though. There were many places which were almost vertical, in which we had to cut steps. Up these places we now made zigzags, so that there was comparatively little difficulty in climbing.

"On the first day I had set fire to the cane in order to clear the trail. This fire did not clear much, however. On the second day I was about a quarter of a mile behind the workmen, or rather above them, when suddenly Tomás (the Peruvian soldier mentioned above), who was with me, said: 'Look, they have fired the cane.'

Sure enough, they had started it, and in a minute it had gained headway and was roaring up toward us, the flames reaching 15 or 20 feet into the air.

ESCAPE FROM FIRE
IN THE JUNGLE

"There was nothing for us but to run, and we did that, tearing through the jungle down hill in an effort to get around the side of the fire. Suddenly, on one of my jumps, I didn't stop when I expected to, but kept right on through the air. The brush had masked a nice little 8-foot jump-off, and I got beautifully bumped. In a minute there came a thump, and Tomás landed beside me. It amused me so much to watch him that I forgot all about my own jolted bones. There was nothing broken, however, and we made our way without much more trouble around the fire and fell upon the peons, who were gathered in a bunch, speculating as to where we might be."

Three days later I reached Machu Picchu in company with Dr. Eaton, our osteologist, and Mr. Erdis, who, as archeological engineer, was to have charge of the general work of clearing and excavating the ruins.

Mr. Heald was at once relieved from further duty at Machu Picchu, where he had just begun the work of clearing, and was asked to see whether he could get to the top of the neighboring peak, called "Huayna Picchu," and investigate the story that there were magnificent ruins upon its summit. The same Indian who had originally told me about the ruins at Machu Picchu had repeatedly declared that those on Huayna Picchu were only slightly inferior. Mr. Heald's report of his work on Huayna Picchu runs in part as follows:

"Huayna Picchu, lying to the north of Machu Picchu, and connected with it by a narrow neck, rises some 2,500 feet above the Urubamba River, which runs around its base. On one side, the south, this elevation is reached by what is practically one complete precipice. On the other, while there are sheer ascents, there are also slopes, and, according to the account of one Arteaga, who claims to have explored the forests which cover a good deal of it, was once cultivated, the slopes being converted into level fields by low earth terraces.

ATTEMPT AT SCALING
HUAYNA PICCHU

"This mountain is, like Machu Picchu, cut from medium-grained gray to red granite, which accounts in part for its sharp, craggy outlines. The lower slopes, where there are any, are covered with forest growths of large trees. A peculiar thing in this connection is one solitary palm tree, which rises above the other vegetation. Near the top the large trees give place to cane and mesquite, while many slopes have nothing but grass. This last is due more to steepness and lack of soil than to any peculiarity of elevation or location, however. . . .

"My first trip to reach the summit of Huayna Picchu and to ascertain what ruins, if any, were on it, ended in failure. The only man who had been up (Arteaga), who lives at Mandor Pampa, was drunk, and refused to go with me; so I decided to try to find a way without his help. I knew where his bridge crossed the Urubamba River and where he had started up when he went the year before. With these two things to help me, I thought that I could very likely find as much as he had. Accordingly, I started with four peons and Tomás Cobines, the soldier, to have a look.

EXCAVATING AT MACHU PICCHU

Commencing the work of excavating in the Chief Temple at Machu Picchu. Lieutenant Sotomayor, at the right, in charge of the gang of Indians.

A BURIAL CAVE AT MACHU PICCHU

The first burial cave discovered at Machu Picchu containing a human skull. The picture was taken after partial excavation, showing the skull still in place. In all, more than 100 such caves were opened and a large quantity of skeletal material secured.

A LARGE BURIAL CAVE: MACHU PICCHU

A flashlight view of cave No. 9, one of the larger burial caves, in the floor of which a number of skeletons were found. On the ground among the rocks were pieces of beautiful large pots, which may have been destroyed at the time of burial.

COLLECTING THE SKELETAL REMAINS OF THE ANCIENT INHABITANTS: MACHU PICCHU

A flashlight view of the interior of cave No. 11, showing the osteologist, Dr. Eaton, and his Indian helpers during the excavation of a human skeleton. The man at the right is a soldier kindly loaned to us by the Peruvian government to assist us in securing laborers.

32

Photo by Hiram Bingham

THE LARGEST CAVE AT MACHU PICCHU

A flashlight view of the interior of the largest cave, at the base of one of the great precipices of Huayna Picchu. The cave is nearly 90 feet in length and is partly lined with cut stones. It had long been known to the Indian treasure-hunters of the neighborhood, and consequently yielded no results.

Photo by Hiram Bingham

THE TEMPLE OF THE THREE WINDOWS: MACHU PICCHU

The floors of the principal temples yielded little, but on the terraces beneath the walls of the three-windowed temple, here shown, we found potsherds and artifacts to a depth of four or five feet.

Photo by Hiram Bingham

MACHU PICCHU AFTER TEN DAYS' CLEARING

General view of the west side of Machu Picchu, showing our camp in the upper left-hand corner and a portion of the city after ten days of clearing. Under the old tropical forest was one of the most important portions of the city. The effect of clearing this forest is shown in the next picture.

Photo by Hiram Bingham

MACHU PICCHU A MONTH LATER

A nearer view of the same place one month later, showing the terraces of the upper city and the rows of windowed houses that had been hidden for centuries beneath the tropical forest.

Photo by Hiram Bingham

A STAGE IN THE CLEARING OF MACHU PICCHU

Our first camp is just visible at the top of the picture. The buildings in the foreground belong to what was called the Ingenuity Group. The picture was taken during the preliminary clearing.

ONE OF THE MAGNIFICENT PRECIPICES
WHICH MADE THE CITY OF MACHU PICCHU INVULNERABLE

"The river was passed easily on the rather shaky four-pole bridge, and we started up the slope, cutting steps as we went, for it was almost vertical. About 30 feet up it moderated, however, and, after that, while it was steep, we seldom had to cut steps for more than 20 to 30 feet on a stretch. The greatest hindrance was the cane and long grass, through which it was hard to cut a way with the machetes.

"Our progress, slow at first, got absolutely snail-like as the men got tired; so, getting impatient, I resolved to push on alone, telling them to follow the marks of my machete, and charging Tomás to see that they made a good trail and did not loaf.

"I pushed on up the hill, clearing my way with the machete, or down on all fours, following a bear trail (of which there were many), stopping occasionally to open my shirt at the throat and cool off, as it was terribly hot. The brush through which I made my way was in great part mesquite, terribly tough and with heavy, strong thorns. If a branch was not cut through at one blow, it was pretty sure to come

Photo by Hiram Bingham

THE NARROW RIDGE ON WHICH MACHU PICCHU IS SITUATED AND THE MAGNIFICENT URUBAMBA CAÑON

A distant view of Machu Picchu on its narrow ridge, flanked by precipices, in the most inaccessible corner of the Andes in the heart of the Urubamba Cañon. The sharp peak in the right foreground is Machu Picchu Mountain. The lower conical peak at the extreme left is Huayna Picchu. The city of Machu Picchu is on top of the ridge between these two peaks and almost directly underneath the little fleecy cloud which hides part of a distant mountain.

Photo by Hiram Bingham

THE OUTER CITY WALL: MACHU PICCHU

The defenses of Machu Picchu consisted of two walls and a dry moat running across the ridge from precipice to precipice. In this picture may be seen the outer wall and the ruins of buildings probably used by the soldiers who protected the outer defenses.

Photo by Hiram Bingham

THE INNER WALL AND THE CITY GATE: MACHU PICCHU

By building this wall forward from the gate, it was possible to direct a lateral fire on besiegers. Ammunition consisted of stones—large ones which could be thrown down on the heads of an attacking force, and small cobble stones brought up from the river 2,000 feet below to be used in slings. Piles of this selected ammunition were found in various parts of the defenses.

whipping back and drive half a dozen spikes into hands, arms, and body. Luckily I had had enough practice to learn how to strike with a heavy shoulder blow, and for the most part made clean strokes, but I didn't get away untouched by any means.

A NARROW ESCAPE

"Finally, about 3 p. m., I had almost gained the top of the lowest part of the ridge, which runs along like the backplates of some spined dinosaur. The trees had given way to grass or bare rock, the face of the rock being practically

THE WESTERN TERRACES AND THE STEEP WINDING STAIRWAY: MACHU PICCHU

It was difficult to feed the thousands of people who at one time may have occupied Machu Picchu, and every square foot of available land was terraced off to provide a place for the crops of Indian corn and potatoes, which were their chief resource. These terraces were all connected by stairways, sometimes steep, narrow, and winding like the one on the left, at other times consisting of a row of projecting stones in the face of the terrace, as is the case in the second terrace below the lowest line of niches in this picture.

AN ANCIENT SIGNAL STATION ON MACHU PICCHU MOUNTAIN

On the very summit of one of the most stupendous precipices the Incas constructed a signal station from which the approach of an enemy could be instantly communicated to the city below. By looking very carefully the terraced walls of this signal station may be seen just below the figures who are standing on an artificial platform.

vertical. A cliff some 200 feet high stood in my way. By going out to the end of the ridge I thought I could look almost straight down to the river, which looked more like a trout-brook than a river at that distance, though its roar in the rapids came up distinctly.

"I was just climbing out on the top of the lowest 'back-plate' when the grass and soil under my feet let go, and I dropped. For about 20 feet there was a slope of about 70 degrees, and then a jump of about 200 feet, after which it would be bump and repeat down to the river.

"As I shot down the sloping surface I reached out and with my right hand grasped a mesquite bush that was growing in a crack about 5 feet above the jump-off. I was going so fast that it jerked my arm up, and, as my body was turning, pulled me from my side to my face; also, the jerk broke the ligaments holding the outer ends of the clavicle and scapula together. The strength left the arm with the tearing loose of the ligaments, but I had checked enough to give me a chance to get hold of a branch with my left hand.

"After hanging for a moment or two, so as to look everything over, and be sure that I did nothing wrong, I started to work back up. The hardest part was to get my feet on the trunk of the little tree to which I was holding on. The fact that I was wearing moccasins instead of boots helped a great deal here, as they would take hold of the rock. It was distressingly slow work, but after about half an hour I had gotten back to comparatively safe footing. As my right

Photo by Hiram Bingham

A NEARER VIEW OF THE PLATFORM SKILFULLY CONSTRUCTED ON TOP OF MACHU PICCHU MOUNTAIN 4,000 FEET ABOVE THE RIVER IN THE VALLEY BELOW

THE DRY MOAT OF THE DEFENSES OF MACHU PICCHU

Just outside the inner walls of Machu Picchu the builders constructed a dry moat which ran directly across the hill. In this picture of the moat the city walls may be seen above on the right and the agricultural terraces on the left.

arm was almost useless, I at once made my way down, getting back to camp about 5.30, taking the workmen with me as I went.

"On this trip I saw no sign of Inca work, except one small ruined wall. . . ."

SUCCESS AT THE THIRD ATTEMPT

Five days later Mr. Heald judged that his arm was in sufficiently good shape so that he could continue the work, and he very pluckily made another attempt to reach the top of Huayna Picchu. This likewise ended in failure; but on the following day he returned to the attack, followed his old trail up some 1,700 feet, and, guided by the same half-breed who had told us about the ruins, eventually reached the top. His men were obliged to cut steps in the steep slope for a part of the distance, until they came to some of stone stairs, which led them practically to the summit.

The top consisted of a jumbled mass of granite boulders about 2,500 feet above the river. There were no houses, though there were several flights of steps and three little caves. No family could have wished to live there. It might have been a signal station.

After Mr. Heald had left Machu Picchu we set ourselves to work to see whether excavation in the principal structures would lead to discovery of any sherds or artifacts. It did not take us long to discover that there were potsherds outside of and beneath the outer walls of several of the important structures, but our digging inside the walls of the principal temples was almost without any results whatsoever. We did find that the floor of the principal temple had been carefully made of a mixture of granite gravel, sand, and clay, laid on top of small stones, and these again on top of a mass of granite rocks and boulders. When the temple was

Photo by Hiram Bingham

A HUGE ROCK IN THE DEFENSES OF MACHU PICCHU

The moat is still from 6 to 8 feet deep, but has probably been partly filled up by the accumulations of centuries. In places unusually large rocks were used in the construction of the inner wall of the moat.

in use this clean, white floor must have been an attractive feature.

THE FIRST EXCAVATIONS

Our workmen excavated with a will, for the tests made with a crowbar gave such resound-

Photo by Hiram Bingham

THE DEFENSES OF MACHU PICCHU:
THE INNER WALL

Besides the moat, the inner defenses of Machu Picchu consisted of a high wall strongly built of large,
rough boulders. The Incas were good engineers and
thoroughly understood the art of drainage. In this picture of the wall may be seen two outlets for water,
permitting the terraces within the wall to be properly drained.

ing hollow sounds that they felt sure there was
treasure to be found beneath the floor of the ancient temple. In places the excavation was carried to a depth of 8 or 9 feet, and practically

the entire floor of the temple was excavated to
a depth of 3 or 4 feet; but all this back-break-
ing work ended only in disappointment. There
were many crevices and holes between the boulders under the floor, but nothing in them—not
even a bone or potsherd.

Digging in the temple of the Three Windows had a similar negative result, but digging outside on the terrace below the three
windows resulted in a large quantity of decorated potsherds. Most of them were 2 to 4 feet
under the surface. It seemed as though it had
been the custom for a long period of time to
throw earthenware out of the windows of this
edifice.

At the end of a week of hard and continuous labor we had not succeeded in finding a
single skull, a single burial cave, nor any pieces
of bronze or pots worth mentioning. We did
not like to resort to the giving of prizes at such
an early stage. A day or two spent in hunting
over the mountain side with the Indians for
burial caves yielding no results, we finally
offered a prize of one sol (50 cents gold) to any
workman who would report the whereabouts of
a cave containing a skull, and who would leave
the cave exactly as he found it, allowing us to
see the skull actually in position.

THE SEARCH
FOR BURIAL CAVES

The next day all the workmen were allowed
to follow their own devices, and they started out
early on a feverish hunt for burial caves. The
half dozen worthies whom we had brought with
us from Cuzco returned at the end of the day
tattered and torn, sadder and no wiser. They
had hewed their way through the jungle, one
of them had cut open his big toe with his ma-

THE DEFENSES OF MACHU PICCHU: THE INNER WALL AND THE CITY GATE

The main city gate of Machu Picchu was on the very summit of the ridge. Its defense was made easy by bringing the wall out in a salient angle on the left of the gate, so that a perfect shower of stones could be rained on the heads of besiegers. The peak in the distance is Huayna Picchu.

chete, their clothes were in shreds, and they had found nothing.

But the Indians who lived in the vicinity, and who had undoubtedly engaged in treasure-hunting before, responded nobly to the offer of a prize, and came back at the end of the day with the story that they had discovered not one, but eight, burial caves, and desired eight soles.

This was the beginning of a highly successful effort to locate and collect the skeletal remains of the ancient inhabitants of Machu Picchu. Fifty-two graves in and near this ancient city were excavated by Dr. Eaton, our osteologist, and fully as many more were afterward located and explored under the supervision of Mr. Erdis, the archeological engineer. The greatest number of these graves were in caves under the large boulders and projecting ledges of the mountain side, and the method usually followed by the osteologist in exploring them was, first, to photograph the entrance of the cave from without, after which the grave was opened and its contents carefully removed. Measurements were taken and diagrams were made to show the position of the human skeletons and the arrangement of the accompanying pottery, implements, ornaments, and bones of lower animals.

In a few instances it was possible also to photograph the interiors of graves.

CONTENTS OF THE BURIAL CAVES

In some of the caves only the most fragmentary skeletal remains were found; in others only the larger bones and a skull or two; while others contained not only nearly complete skeletons, but pots in more or less perfect state of preservation, and occasionally pieces of bronze. In this way a large and valuable collection was made of human skeletons, pottery, and other artifacts of various materials, including some of the tools probably used by the Inca or pre-Inca stone-masons in the more intricate parts of their work.

Before dismissing the subject of the ancient graves, it may be noted that the custom seems to have been, whenever possible, to bury

Photo by Hiram Bingham

A TUNNEL UNDER THE MAIN ROAD:
MACHU PICCHU

The road from the outer world to the city of Machu
Picchu was a well-made footpath about 4 feet wide.
It crosses the agricultural terraces. In the place shown
in the picture, the workmen had constructed a tunnel underneath this road, so as to pass more quickly
from the upper to the lower terraces.

the dead in the sitting position, with the knees
raised. In a very few instances bodies were in-
terred in crudely fashioned "bottle-shaped
graves." While engaged in this work the
collectors were greatly annoyed by the venom-
ous serpents of the region, and several of

these serpents were killed and preserved in alcohol.

The burial caves occur generally on the
sides of the mountain below the ruins. As they
are in well nigh inaccessible locations and more
or less covered with dense tropical jungle, the
work of visiting and excavating them was extremely arduous, and it is most highly to the
credit of those engaged in it that so many caves
were opened and so much material gathered.
Practically every square rod of the sides of the
ridge was explored. The last caves that were
opened were very near the Urubamba River itself, where the ancient laborers may have had
their huts.

It is too early as yet to give any generaliza-
tions with regard to the anatomical characteristics of the Machu Picchu people as evidenced
by their skeletal remains. A few of the skulls
show decided marks of artificial deformation,
but most of them are normal.

Mr. Erdis eventually made the discovery
that by digging at least 18 inches underground,
at the mouths of small caves, under large boulders, within 200 yards of the Three Window
Temple, he was almost sure to find one or two
articles of bronze, either pins, tweezers, pen-
dants, or other ornaments.

Selecting two of the most reliable workmen and offering them a sliding scale of re-
wards for everything they might find of value,
he succeeded, in the course of four months'
faithful attention to the details of clearing and
excavating, in getting together about 200 little
bronzes, a lesser number of pots, and 50 cases
of sherds. The nature of the more interesting
finds can be better understood by the accompanying photograph. This material is now all in
New Haven, where it is to be arranged by Dr.
Eaton and Mr. Erdis.

THE MAIN ROAD TO MACHU PICCHU

Photo by Hiram Bingham

A nearer view of the graded approach to Machu Picchu; part of the principal road which connected the city with the outer world.

WHAT CLEARING THE JUNGLE REVEALED

The change made in the appearance of Machu Picchu by the four months of clearing and excavating is graphically brought out by comparing the pictures with the one set taken either before the work began or early in its stages and the latter taken at the end of the season. It is most sincerely to be hoped that the Peruvian government will not allow the ruins to be overgrown with a dense forest, as they have been in the past.

Although the buildings are extremely well built, there is no cement or mortar in the masonry, and there is no means of preventing the roots of forest trees from penetrating the walls and eventually tearing them all down. In several cases we found gigantic trees perched on the very tips of the gable ends of small and beautifully constructed houses. It was not the least difficult part of our work to cut down and get such trees out of the way without seriously damaging the house walls.

Considering all the pains that we took to preserve the ruins from further spoliation by the dense vegetation, it was with frank and painful surprise that we read in the decree issued by the new Peruvian government, in connection with giving us permission to take out of Peru what we had found, a clause stating that we were not to injure the ruins in the slightest particular, and

THE DEFENSES OF THE CITY: THE NORTHERN TERRACES, MACHU PICCHU

On the north side of the city there was little danger of attack, but in order to strengthen the nearly impassible cliffs and precipices, narrow terraces that could be used both for agricultural and defensive purposes were constructed.

48

A STAIRWAY ON THE MAIN STREET IN MACHU PICCHU

Within the city an extensive system of narrow streets and granite stairways made intercommunication relatively easy. This stairway is on the main cross street which connects the vicinity of the Sacred Plaza and the chief temples with the east city.

Photo by Hiram Bingham

A TYPICAL DWELLING HOUSE OF THE BETTER CLASS: MACHU PICCHU

One of the most striking characteristics of Machu Picchu architecture is that a large majority of the houses are of a story and half in height, with gable ends. These gables are marked by cylindrical projecting stones. carrying out the idea of the wooden rafters, which have disappeared. In the case of these two adjoining houses, the southern gables alone are still standing, the northern gables having been knocked off either by earthquakes or owing to the destructive forest vegetation. Had we not cleared the jungle and cut off the forest trees, the right gable would soon have gone with the weight of the tree that was perched on its peak, and whose roots can still be seen in the picture.

that we must neither deface nor mutilate them. I could not help being reminded of the fact that we had spent two days of one workman's time in erasing from the beautiful granite walls the crude charcoal autographs of visiting Peruvians, one of whom had taken the pains to scrawl in huge letters his name in thirty-three places in the principal and most attractive buildings.

We were greatly aided in the work of clearing the ruins by having with us for two months Lieutenant Sotomayor, of the Peruvian army, whose presence was due to the courtesy of President Leguia. Lieutenant Sotomayor took personal charge of the gang of Indians engaged in clearing the jungle and drying and burning the rubbish. As long as he was allowed to remain with us he did his work most faithfully and efficiently. It was with regret that we found he was relieved from duty at Machu Picchu in September.

AN IDEAL PLACE OF REFUGE

Although it is too early to speak definitely in regard to the civilization of Machu Picchu, a short description of the principal characteristics of the city may not be out of place.

Machu Picchu is essentially a city of refuge. It is perched on a mountain top in the most inaccessible corner of the most inaccessible section of the Urubamba River. So far as I know, there is no part of the Andes that has been better defended by nature.

A stupendous cañon, where the principal rock is granite and where the precipices are frequently over 1,000 feet *sheer*, presents difficulties of attack and facilities for defense second to none. Here on a narrow ridge, flanked on all sides by precipitous or nearly precipitous slopes, a highly civilized people—artistic, inventive, and capable of sustained endeavor—at some time in the remote past built themselves a city of refuge.

Since they had no iron or steel tools—only stone hammers—its construction must have cost many generations, if not centuries, of effort.

Photo by Hiram Bingham

A DECORATED GABLE: MACHU PICCHU

A slightly different view of the gable end of one of the better houses, bringing out the location and size of the projecting cylindrical blocks.

Across the ridge, and defending the builders from attack on the side of the main mountain range, they constructed two walls. One of them, constituting the outer line of defense, leads from precipice to precipice, utilizing as best it can the natural steepness of the hill.

Beyond this, and on top of the mountain called Machu Picchu, which overlooks the valley from the very summit of one of the most stupendous precipices in the cañon, is con-

Photo by Hiram Bingham

THE WEST GABLE IN THE BEST HOUSE OF THE KINGS GROUP

Showing the second story window, a small ventilating window above it, the usual projecting cylinders, and the location of four ring-stones to which the rafters were tied. The ring-stones are located at regular distances. The holes in the stones were probably bored by means of pieces of bamboo, sand, water, a pair of good hands, considerable time, and a great deal of patience.

structed a signal station, from which the approach of an enemy could be instantly communicated to the city below. Within the outer wall they constructed an extensive series of agricultural terraces, stone lined and averaging about 8 feet high. Between these and the city is a steep, dry moat and the inner wall.

When the members of an attacking force had safely negotiated the precipitous and easily defended sides of the moat, they would still find themselves outside the inner defenses of the city, which consisted of a wall from 15 to 20 feet high, composed of the largest stones that could be found in the vicinity—many of them huge boulders weighing many tons. This wall is carried straight across the ridge from one precipitous side to the other. These defenses are on the south side of the city.

THE TOWN WAS INVULNERABLE

On the north side, on the narrow ridge connecting the city with Huayna Picchu, strong defensive terraces have been strategically placed so as to render *nil* the danger of an attack on this side. Difficult to reach at best, the city's defenses were still further strengthened by the construction of high, steep walls wherever the precipices did not seem absolutely impassable.

Inside the city the houses are crowded close together, but an extensive system of narrow streets and rock-hewn stairways made intercommunication comfortable and easy.

On entering the city, perhaps the first characteristic that strikes one is that a large majority of the houses were a story and a half in height, with gable ends, and that these gable ends are marked by cylindrical blocks projecting out from the house in such a way as to suggest the idea of the ends of the rafters. The

wooden rafters have all disappeared, but the ring-stones to which they were tied may still be seen in some of the pictures.

These ring-stones consist of a slab of granite, about 2 feet long and 6 inches wide by 2 inches thick, with a hole bored in one end, and were set into the sloping gable wall in such a way as to be flush with the surface, although the hole was readily accessible for lashing the beams of the house to the steep pitch of the gables. There were usually four of these ring-stones on each slope of the wall. Dr. Eaton found this to be also a feature of the Choqquequirau architecture, only in that city the number of ring-stones is larger per gable.

A CITY OF STAIRWAYS

The next most conspicuous feature of Machu Picchu is the quantity of stairways, there being over 100, large and small, within the city. Some of them have more than 150 steps, while others have but 3 or 4. In some cases each step is a single block of stone 3 or 4 feet wide. In others the entire stairway—6, 8, or 10 steps, as the case might be—was cut out of a single granite boulder.

Again, the stairway would seem almost fantastic, being so narrow and wedged in between two boulders so close together that it would have been impossible for a fat man to use the stairway at all. In no case were the stairways intended for ornament. In every case they are useful in getting to a location otherwise difficult of access.

The largest level space in the city was carefully graded and terraced, so as to be used for agricultural purposes, on the products of which the inhabitants could fall back for a time in case of a siege.

A WELL-BUILT GRANITE STAIRWAY:
MACHU PICCHU

Apart from the unusual number of windows in the houses of Machu Picchu, the most remarkable thing is the number of granite stairways, there being over 100, large and small, within the walls of the city. This is a portion of one of the more important stairways on one of the principal streets in the city.

It seems probable that one reason why the city was deserted was a change in climate, resulting in scarcity of water supply. At the present time there are only three small springs on the mountain-side, and in the dry season

ANOTHER MONOLITHIC STAIRWAY:
MACHU PICCHU

In this case not only the steps of the stairway but also the balustrades, were cut out of a single stone. Imagine the patience required to do this, when the only tools at hand were hard cobble stones that had to be brought up from the river 2,000 feet below.

these could barely furnish water enough for cooking and drinking purposes for 40 or 50 people. There could never have been very much water here, for the *azequias*, or water channels, are narrower than any we have ever seen anywhere else, being generally less than 4 inches in width.

Photo by Hiram Bingham

THE STEEPEST STAIRWAY IN MACHU PICCHU

This stairway is one of those connecting the various agricultural terraces, and as it was in a position where it was not needed to be used for constant traffic, as in the streets of the city, it was left to follow the extremely steep natural declivity of the hill.

THE FOUNTAINS ON THE STAIRWAY

We were able to trace the principal *azequia* from the vicinity of the springs along the mountain-side for a distance of perhaps a mile, across the dry moat on a slender bridge, then under the city wall, along one of the terraces, and finally to the first of a series of fountains or baths, located on the principal stairway of the city.

This stairway is divided to admit the entrance of one of the fountains, of which there are 14 or 15 in the series. Each basin is about 2½ feet long by 1½ feet wide and from 5 to 6 inches in depth. In some cases the basin and the floor of the bath-house, or fountain, is made of a single slab of granite. Generally holes were drilled in one of the corners of the basin to permit the water to flow through carefully cut underground channels to the next basin below.

The Peruvians call these fountains "baths." It does not seem to me likely that they were used for this purpose, but rather that, by a careful husbanding in basins of this sort, the water-pots of the inhabitants could the more readily be filled by any one coming to one of the fountains.

Many of the houses are built on terraces on the steep sloping hillsides. In such case their doors face the hill and the windows look out on the view. Most of the houses are well provided with niches, the average size being about 2 feet in height by 1¼ feet in width. In some interi-

Photo by Hiram Bingham

THE STAIRWAY OF THE FOUNTAINS: MACHU PICCHU

The longest and most important stairway is so arranged as to admit the entrance of fountains, of which there are 14 or 15 in a series. As they had no pipes, the builders conducted the water in skillfully made stone conduits, carrying the stream from basin to basin, sometimes under the stairway and sometimes at its side.

Photo by Hiram Bingham

A FOUNTAIN AT MACHU PICCHU

Fountain showing the opening of the conduit. Owing to a change in climate, the springs which formerly fed these fountains are now so small as to give scarcely water enough for three families, except in the wet season.

Photo by Hiram Bingham

INTERIOR OF ONE OF THE BEST HOUSES: MACHU PICCHU

Houses with more than one room were scarce, but where this does occur, the doors, as in the picture, are very small.

ors projecting cylindrical blocks are found alternating between the niches. In a few houses we found evidence of stucco, but in most cases the mud plaster had entirely disappeared.

Possibly the most interesting conclusion brought out as a result of our extensive clearing and excavating is that the city was at one time divided into wards or clan groups. Each one of these groups has but one entrance, a gateway furnished with the means of being solidly fastened on the inside. None of the doors to houses or temples have this locking device, but all the entrances to the clan groups have it, and the same device occurs in the principal gate to the city.

Photo by Hiram Bingham

TYPICAL INTERIOR OF SMALL CHAMBER IN BETTER CLASS HOUSE: MACHU PICCHU

Most of the houses are well provided with niches, the average size being about 2 feet in height and a foot and a quarter in width. These niches took the place of closets, wardrobes, shelves, and tables. They were usually symmetrically arranged and offered a pleasing break in the dull finish of the solid walls.

ANOTHER TYPICAL INTERIOR: MACHU PICCHU Photo by Hiram Bingham

In many of the houses there are round or square stones projecting between the niches. In some cases these were used to support an upper story, while in other cases they are either for ornament or merely convenient hooks on which to hang ponchos, slings, ropes, etc.

58

STUCCO STILL IN POSITION: MACHU PICCHU   Photo by Hiram Bingham

Some of the houses were lined with such beautiful stone work as to require no other finish. In others it seems probable that the roughly finished stones were covered with some kind of mud or plaster. The picture shows the only house in Machu Picchu where considerable portions of this plaster still remain on the walls.

INGENIOUS BOLTING OF THE GATES TO THE CLAN GROUPS

The doors have disappeared, but probably consisted of rough-hewn logs of hard wood. They seem to have been fastened by two bars crossed at right angles. The upright bar was probably tied at the top to a ring-stone set in the wall and projecting from it above the stone lintel of the doorway. It could have been fastened at the bottom by being set into a shallow hole in the ground. The cross-bar was lashed to stone cylinders about 6 inches high and 3 inches in diameter, set into lock-holes in the door-posts.

This ingenious device varies in different groups, but in general the principle is the same.

The more common method of making these locks was to cut a hole out of the top or corner of one of the larger blocks in the door-posts and set the stone cylinder into saucer-shaped depressions below and above. Thus the cylinder would be so firmly keyed into the wall that it would be able to resist at least as much pressure as the hardwood cross-bar which was lashed to it.

Each one of the clan groups has certain distinctive features. In one of them, characterized by particularly ingenious stone-cutting, the lock-holes were cut in the center of solid granite rectangular blocks. The picture, taken after the top block had been removed, shows the saucer-shaped depression cut into the upper stone.

It also explains how the ingenious architect had carved the cylindrical block and the lock-hole all out of one piece, thus making it much stronger than the average.

Granite boulders in the floor of the principal house in this group had their tops carved into kitchen-utensils for grinding corn and frozen potatoes. In this group also we found the only case of houses lined with stucco or plaster made of red clay, and here is the only gabled building divided into two parts by a party wall rising to the peak and pierced by three windows.

SOME EXQUISITE STONEWORK

Another group was distinguished by having its own private gardens on terraces so arranged that access to them could be had only by passing through the small collection of houses constituting this particular clan group. In another case, the entrance to a group notable for its very elaborate and exquisitely finished stonework, the upright cylinder in the lock-hole is brought flush with the surface of the stone and is a part of the block itself.

Photo by Hiram Bingham

THE LOCK IN THE CITY GATE: MACHU PICCHU

A nearer view of one of the lock-holes in the east door-post of the city gate.

Photo by Hiram Bingham

TYPICAL HOUSES AT MACHU PICCHU

This picture shows a part of the east portion of the city and the entrances to clan groups. One of the principal streets in the city runs along the terrace just outside the walls of the houses.

THE CITY GATE: MACHU PICCHU

Photo by Hiram Bingham

The doors to the houses had apparently no means of being fastened, but the entrances to the clan groups and the main city gate, whose interior is here shown, had lock-holes containing granite cylinders to which a strong bar could be fastened back of the gate. The ring-stone above the stone lintel at the top of the picture was used to secure the upright bar.

THIS DRAWING OF A SECTION OF THE
CITY WALL AND THE CITY GATE SHOWS
HOW THE STONE CYLINDERS WERE SET
INTO THE GATE-POSTS

AN IMAGINARY DRAWING
SHOWING HOW THE CITY GATE
MIGHT HAVE BEEN CLOSED

Photo by Hiram Bingham

ONE OF THE WARDS OR CLAN GROUPS INTO WHICH THE CITY WAS ONCE DIVIDED

The city of Machu Picchu was occupied by various clans or family groups. Each one of them has from six to ten houses, and each group of houses is characterized by some peculiarity. In the case of the group shown in the picture, this peculiarity consists of particularly ingenious stone-cutting, examples of which are shown in the pictures.

62

THE MOST INGENIOUS LOCK IN MACHU PICCHU

Photo by Hiram Bingham

The gateway to Ingenuity Group had lock-holes differing from those of other groups, in that they were cut out of single blocks of stone and had the stone cylinder not set into but forming part of the whole block.

A TYPICAL HOUSE DOOR: MACHU PICCHU

Photo by Hiram Bingham

The doors of the houses were carefully made and are all narrower at the top than at the bottom. The lintels are usually made of two blocks of stone. The Indian boy in the picture is carrying the kodaks and a large map, in ten sheets, on which are shown all the houses.

Another group is distinguished by having monolithic lintels for the doorways. In this group also the gables are unusually steep.

Nearly all the groups had what seemed to be a religious center, consisting of a more or less carved granite block in position. In several cases

THE MECHANISM OF THE LOCK

The left-hand lock-hole, shown in the upper picture on the preceding page, after its stone covering had been raised, showing the saucer-shaped depression in the capstone, enabling it to strengthen the stone cylinder of the lock. It was not only an ingenious, but a patient and devoted workman, who would take the trouble to make such a contrivance for securing himself and his family against intruders.

A DETAIL OF THE CITY GATE: MACHU PICCHU

Above the gate and fastened into the wall above the stone lintel was a ring-stone from which the gate might have been swung, or to which one of its fastenings might have been secured.

caves had been excavated under these rocks, and in one case the cave was beautifully lined with finely cut stonework. In this last cave a semicircular tower was constructed on the top of a boulder and connected with it by the finest example of masonry in Machu Picchu.

This beautiful wall was made of specially selected blocks of beautifully grained white

Photo by Hiram Bingham

A VIEW IN THE CENTER OF INGENUITY GROUP
LOOKING ACROSS THE GARDENS TOWARD THE SACRED PLAZA
AND THE TEMPLE OF THE THREE WINDOWS

granite, and was constructed by a master artist. We grew more fond of this wall the longer we knew it, and every time we saw it it gave us a thrill of joy.

The detailed study of where the wall joins the next house wall shows how ingeniously the blocks were constructed, so as to form a brace which would prevent the house and wall from leaning apart and thus causing cracks to appear in the wall. The precision of line, the symmetrical arrangement of the blocks, and the gradual gradation in the tiers, with the largest at the bottom and the smallest at the top, combine to produce a wonderfully beautiful effect.

THE PROBABLE USE OF SNAKES FOR AUGURY

As will be seen from the photograph, the wall is not perpendicular, but inclines inward at the top. This angle is characteristic of nearly all the vertical lines in the ruins. Doors, windows, and niches are all narrower at the top than at the bottom.

In the semicircular tower which connects with this fine wall the ingenious cutting of stones in such a way as to follow a selected curve reaches a perfection equaled only in the celebrated wall of the Temple of the Sun (now the Dominican Monastery), in Cuzco. Like that it is a flattened curve, not round.

Photo by Hiram Bingham

A REST DURING PRELIMINARY CLEARING: MACHU PICCHU

A corner of Ingenuity Group, showing the entrance on the left to a subsidiary group and on the right to the house that has the stone mortars in its floor.

One of the windows in this tower has several small holes near the bottom. These were found to connect, by very narrow channels, barely large enough for a snake to crawl through, with circular holes within the wall, where the snakes might have constructed their nests.

There are still many snakes at Machu Picchu. There are also snakes carved on several rocks. Lizards are not common, and the holes within the wall are much too large for lizards' nests; but they are of the right size for a comfortable snake's nest—for a small snake. It seems to me possible that in this wall the priest of this clan group kept a few tame snakes and that he used their chance exits out of one hole or another as a means of telling omens and possibly of prophesying.

The so-called *sacred plaza* is the site of two of the finest structures at Machu Picchu. One of these—the Temple of the Three Windows—has already been referred to; the other is a remarkable structure, about 12 feet in height, built around three sides of a rectangle some 30 feet long and 18 feet wide. A description is hardly necessary, as a better idea can be gained from the pictures than from any words of mine. Suffice it to say that it is marked by a very pleasing symmetry, by the use of tremendous blocks of granite, three of them being over 12 feet in length, and by the projection in an obtuse angle of the ends of the sides.

Photo by Hiram Bingham

AN ATTRACTIVE CORNER:
MACHU PICCHU

The entrance hallway to the Princess Group, showing the interior of the gateway, where the upright cylinder in the lock-hole is brought flush with the surface of the door-post.

"THE PLACE TO WHICH
THE SUN IS TIED"

On top of the beautifully terraced hill, behind this temple, is a stone, generally agreed to
be an *intihuatana* stone, or sun-dial—the intihuatana being the "place to which the sun is
tied." Similar stones were found by the Spanish conquerors in Cuzco, Pisac, and Ollantay-

tambo. An idea of this stone may be gained from
the picture.

Owing to the location of Machu Picchu in
this extremely inaccessible part of the Andes, to
its clearly having been a city of refuge, easily defended and suited for defensive purposes;ow-
ing to the presence of a large number of windows in the ruins, and particularly to the
presence of three large windows in one of the
principal temples, I believe it to have been the
original Tampu Tocco, from which the Incas
came when they started on that migration which
led them to conquer Cuzco and to establish the
Inca Empire.

The difficulties of life for several centuries
in the Vilcabamba region would have been likely
to have developed this ingenious and extremely
capable race and given them strength of character. The influence of geographical environ-
ment is no small factor in developing racial
characteristics. I hope at no distant future to
prepare an exhaustive report of this wonderful
city, whose charm can only dimly be realized
from these pictures.

The beautiful blue of the tropical sky, the
varying shades of green that clothe the magnificent mountains, and the mysterious charm of
the roaring rapids thousands of feet below cannot be portrayed and can with difficulty be
imagined.

THE PANORAMIC VIEW

The beautiful panoramic view of Machu
Picchu, which accompanies this article as a
Supplement, gives a good idea of the grand
Cañon of the Urubamba as seen from Machu
Picchu, of the sacred Plaza, and Intihuatana
Hill, and of the East City.

Unfortunately, it was impossible to take a
picture that would also include the other half

Photo by Hiram Bingham

IN THE KING'S GROUP: MACHU PICCHU

A portion of the interior of this group, showing the great care exercised in the stone-fitting.

of Machu Picchu, including the remarkable Upper City, with its rows of houses, each one on a separate terrace, the beautiful buildings of the Princess Group, and the splendid stonework of the King's Group. All of these are behind and to the right of one looking at this panorama. And still further behind are the agricultural terraces, our camp, and Machu Picchu Mountain; but these are all shown in separate views.

The Incas were, undeniably, lovers of beautiful scenery. Many of the ruins of their most important places are located on hill tops, ridges, and mountain shoulders from which particularly beautiful views can be obtained.

Remarkable as is the architecture of Machu Picchu, and impressive as is the extent of the stone-cutting done by a people who had no steel or iron tools, neither of these things leaves

Photo by Hiram Bingham

A SACRED ROCK: MACHU PICCHU

Nearly all the clan groups had what seems to have been a religious center, consisting of a granite boulder or ledge carved into seats and platforms.

Photo by Hiram Bingham

ANOTHER SACRED ROCK: MACHU PICCHU

One of these sacred rocks is only 2 feet in thickness, although 15 feet high and 30 feet in length.

69

A SACRED ROCK GROUP SURROUNDED BY TERRACES
FACED WITH EXTRAORDINARILY LARGE ROCKS

It must have required a tremendous amount of ingenuity and a small army of laborers to get these huge rocks fitted into place.

THE INTERIOR OF A CAVE UNDER A SACRED STONE: MACHU PICCHU

Under the sacred stones frequently caves were constructed and in some cases lined with beautifully cut stones. This is a flashlight of such a cave underneath the semicircular tower.

70

Photo by Hiram Bingham

Photo by Hiram Bingham

TIIE CORNER OF THE CAVE

Another flashlight of the interior of the cave under the semicircular tower in the Princess Group.

AN EXTRAORDINARY PIECE OF STONE-FITTING: MACHU PICCHU

The entrance to the cave under the great rock on which rests the semicircular tower. Notice with what exquisite care and precision the space-between the granite ledges has been filled with cut stone.

more impression on the mind of the visitor than the inexpressible beauty and grandeur of the surroundings.

A reconnaissance of the forestration of the immediate vicinity and a large scale map of Machu Picchu and its vicinity were made by Assistant Topographer Stephenson. From the map we hope some day to be able to construct a model which will give those not fortunate

enough to visit this marvelous place some idea of its character and beauty.

FORESTRATION OF THE REGION

In regard to the forestration of the region, Mr. Stephenson reports that tree-growth begins about midway between the source and the mouth of the Urubamba River. Forests fre-

Photo by Hiram Bingham

Photo by Hiram Bingham

INGENIOUS STONE-FITTING:
MACHU PICCHU

A section of the ornamental wall, showing how ingeniously the joint was made with the next house
wall, so as to form a brace which would prevent the
house and ornamental wall from leaning apart. Notice the exquisite precision with which each block,
after all these centuries in a land where earthquakes
are not uncommon, fits snugly into its neighbors.
There is no cement nor mortar, and yet there is
scarcely a place where a pin can be driven between
the stones.

AN EXTRAORDINARY TOWER:
MACHU PICCHU

Another view of the semicircular tower of the Princess Group, showing the flattened curve of its architectural plan. The stones were cut with such precision and followed so exactly the selected curve that
when they were put together they made a flattened
curve whose perfection of detail is equaled only in the
celebrated wall of the Temple of the Sun in Cuzco.

quently interrupted by open areas occupy the
lower half of the valley. The open bottoms are

moist, untimbered, and used for agriculture. In
these the soil is a deep sandy loam, rich in hu-
mus and having abundant moisture.

    The valley is very narrow, with many tribu-
taries, and rough precipitous sides frequently

broken by cliffs. The lower slopes have fairly rich soil and abundant moisture. They extend for several hundred feet above the river. Above them the soil is regularly dry and poor. Although rainfall is abundant, the sunny north slopes have a dry rocky soil.

The forest in the Machu Picchu region is made up of subtropical hardwoods, with probably more than 30 species in the stand. Good growth is confined to the valley bottoms and the lower slopes. On the shaded slopes the forest sometimes extends to a point 2,000 feet above the river, and in narrow, protected valleys even higher; but on the upper slopes the trees are of poor form, gnarled and stunted.

On the ridges some trees occur, but they are very scrubby and do not form a canopy. Timber-line here is at elevation of about 10,000 feet above sea-level. The elevation of the river near Machu Picchu is about 6,500 feet above sea-level.

Owing to the large number of species, the quality of the timber varies greatly. Many of these species produce hard, durable wood of fine texture that takes good polish. Other quick-growing species produce woods of inferior quality—soft, brittle, quickly decaying, and of little value for anything but rough lumber.

NOTES ON THE TIMBER

All species are infected with parasites and all ages of trees seem to be subject to them. The worst damage is done to the fast-growing young trees.

In the bottoms the trees are tall, clean, and straight, running up to over 100 feet in height and 3 feet in diameter. The average is about 18 inches in diameter and 80 feet in height. On the lower slopes the growth is more uniform, with a slightly lower average size. There are a few

Photo by Hiram Bingham

THE FINEST WALL
IN MACHU PICCHU

The exterior of the ornamental wall, the most beautiful wall in Machu Picchu. The tiers of stones gradually decrease in size toward the top of the wall. The utmost care was exercised in selecting the purest white granite, so as to produce an effect like that of the marble temples in the Old World.

healthy patches of timber, but they are only of occasional occurrence and limited to a few areas.

The timber in the valley bottoms averages 5,000 board-feet per acre, with a maximum of 10,000 over limited areas. On the slopes the average is 3,000 board-feet, with little variation. These are conservative ocular estimates.

Photo by Hiram Bingham

IN THE PRINCESS GROUP: MACHU PICCHU

A general view of the Princess Group, showing the relation of the semicircular tower (on the right) to the other houses of the group. In the center of the picture is the only house in Machu Picchu consisting of two stories and a half. The stairway shown in the picture connects the first and second stories of this house.

AN EXAMPLE OF EXTRAORDINARY STONE-CUTTING: MACHU PICCHU

Connected with the semicircular tower is an ornamental wall made of specially selected blocks of beautifully grained white granite. The interior of the wall was ornamented by a series of symmetrical niches, between each one of which is a projecting stone roughly squared.

REMARKABLE NICHES AT MACHU PICCHU

Another portion of the interior of the ornamental wall. Bear in mind that the ancient builders had no T squares nor right lines, and could approach straight lines only by the skill of a trained eye.

75

A SIGHTLY TOWER: MACHU PICCHU   Photo by Hiram Bingham

The corner of the Princess Group where the ornamental wall joins the semicircular tower is one of the most sightly spots in the city and commands a magnificent view of the great cañon. Within the tower was a sacred rock, which has been partly destroyed by fire.

The rugged character of the country makes logging of any but timber in bottoms impracticable. Trails are few and very bad; labor is scarce and uncertain. Should a railroad enter the valley as planned it will be possible to carry on profitable logging operations with portable mills. There is a good supply of timber for ties.

The next thing to be done would be to make a collection of samples, so that the qualities of the various hardwoods might be tested. Such tests would bring out definite facts about their value. Some of them are undoubtedly woods of high technical qualities as well as of beautiful grade and color.

Mr. Stevenson's map of Machu Picchu, the result of a three months' survey, is on a scale of 1 inch = 20 feet, with a contour interval of 10 feet, and consists of 16 large sheets. It should prove very useful in helping us to gain a correct idea of this wonderful city, which seems to have escaped the notice of the Spanish conquerors and to have remained practically unknown until it was first visited by the present writer in July, 1911.

OTHER IMPORTANT INCA RUINS

It is still too early to make definite statements in regard to the importance of this discovery; in fact, such opinions can only be passed by archeological experts after the full report of the work at Machu Picchu has been prepared and published. This much, however, can be said

REMARKABLE MASONRY AT MACHU PICCHU

The semicircular tower and the interior of the ornamental wall looking toward the steep gables of the King's Group and the stairway near Private Garden Group.

THE PRINCESS GROUP: MACHU PICCHU

A general view of the ornamental wall and the semicircular tower, together with the second story of the adjoining house, looking toward the principal agricultural terraces and our camp in the distance.

77

Photo by Hiram Bingham

THE SNAKE WINDOW: MACHU PICCHU

In the flat wall of the semicircular tower is a remarkable window containing holes leading to little passages in the wall through which snakes might pass to chambers left inside the wall in which they might have their nests. In the Temple of the Sun, in Cuzco, which is characterized also by having a semicircular building, holes similar to these have also been found, and it is presumable that there are inner chambers also in that wall.

in regard to the superiority in extent and interest of Machu Picchu over previously discovered Inca ruins:

The most important Inca ruins heretofore discovered are in the city of Cuzco, the town and fortress of Ollantaytambo, Pisac, and on the islands of Lake Titicaca. There are, besides these, on the coast a number of localities like Pachacamác, Nazca, Ancon, Trujillo, and the country of the Grand Chimu, where the chief interest lies in the extensive findings of mummies, pottery, textiles, and metal ornaments, including gold, silver, bronze, etc. All of these places, however, were known to the Spanish Conquerors, and have been ransacked by treasure hunters from the earliest times.

Cuzco, the most important place of all, was adopted by the Spaniards as their most important city outside of Lima. They entirely remade the city, using large quantities of the ancient Inca walls to build their own palaces and churches. Although the city still has many Inca remains and retains a great charm for the tourist and the archeological student, it is more of a Spanish colonial city than of an Inca city.

The same is partly true of Ollantaytambo. The ruins of Pisac and many others in the vicinity, of which it is not necessary to give an account here, have repeatedly been ransacked by treasure hunters. The long palace at Vitcos, identified in 1911 as the last Inca capital, has been almost completely destroyed by these treasure hunters. Of the 30 beautiful door of cut granite, only two or three remain intact.

WHY MACHU PICCHU IS AN ARCHEOLOGICAL TREASURE

On the other hand, Machu Picchu not only is larger and contains more edifices than any other ruin discovered in Peru (except Cuzco); it has the additional advantage of not having been known to the Spaniards, of not having been occupied by their descendants, and of not having been torn to pieces by treasure hunters seeking within the walls for the gold and silver ornaments that were not to be found in the floors.

Photo by Hiram Bingham

ANOTHER VIEW OF THE SNAKE WINDOW

Showing very clearly the holes in the wall for the admission of snakes.

THE SNAKE WINDOW FROM WITHIN

Photo by Hiram Bingham

There were several means of exit from each snake nest, and it is possible that the priest of this temple attempted to fortell the future by noticing from which holes the snakes chanced to come out.

THE INTERIOR OF THE SEMICIRCULAR TOWER NEAR THE SNAKE WINDOW

The cracks in the walls were probably caused by a great conflagration centuries ago.

SNAKE ROCK: MACHU PICCHU

Photo by Hiram Bingham

On top of one of the boulders near the Sacred Plaza there are several snakes carved into the surface of the rock. The carving of snakes on rocks seems to have been common among prehistoric peoples all over the world.

SUN ROCK: MACHU PICCHU

Photo by Hiram Bingham

On another curiously broken stone is carved a sun, several small snakes, and a few undecipherable figures.

THE PRINCESS GROUP: MACHU PICCHU

The semicircular tower containing the snake window and its immediate surroundings, showing the principal houses of the Princess Group on the left, the stairway of the fountains on the right, and the King's Group at the extreme right.

AN ARCHITECTURAL TRIUMPH: MACHU PICCHU

A general view of the Sacred Plaza, the site of the finest structures at Machu Picchu. In the center is the Chief Temple, and at the right the Temple of the Three Windows. Above them is the Sacred Hill, on top of which is the Intihuatana stone, or sun dial. Contrast this picture, which was taken in 1912, after months of strenuous work in cleaning the city, with the picture on the following page, which was taken in 1911.

Photo by H. L. Tucker

A PICTURE OF THE SAME PART OF THE CITY OF MACHU PICCHU AS SHOWN IN THE
PRECEDING ILLUSTRATION, BUT PHOTOGRAPHED THE YEAR BEFORE

The comparison of these two pictures shows in a very striking manner the immense amount of labor and energy expended by members of the expedition in 1912 in clearing the ruins, so that the members of the National Geographic Society could obtain a good conception of the city.

84

Photo by Hiram Bingham

A CORNER OF THE
THREE-WINDOWED TEMPLE

In the walls of the temples on the Sacred Plaza are
several extraordinarily large granite blocks. In the hole
in the upper left-hand corner of the picture rested one
end of the beam which supported the roof on the west
side of the Temple of the Three Windows. The
women are wives of our workmen. The one on the
right was wearing a green skirt with a red waist and
blue stripes; the one on the left had on a blue skirt
and a red blouse with black dots.

In other words, Machu Picchu is not only
more extensive than any previously discovered

Inca city outside of Cuzco, but it is in a remarkably good state of preservation, and its architecture has not become confused with Spanish efforts to build churches and villas.

If the theory here propounded is correct—
that Machu Picchu was the Original "Tampu
Tocco," from whose "three windows" set out
the tribes that eventually founded Cuzco—
the importance of Machu Picchu as the cradle
of the later Inca race will, of course, be increased.

It is not very profitable to speculate on the
habits of these ancient people until we have had
more opportunity to study the finds made in the
burial caves and to compare these with finds
made in other parts of Peru. We know that they
were masters of the art of stone-cutting.

We know that they knew how to make
bronze, and that they had a considerable artistic sense, as evidenced by their workmanship.
One of the bronze pins found at Machu Picchu
has for a head a miniature reproduction of the
head of a humming-bird, including a long,
curved bill. One bronze knife is decorated with
the head of a llama; another with an Indian boy,
lying on his stomach, with his heels in the air,
playing tug-of-war with a large fish on the end
of a little bronze rope.

The workmen of Machu Picchu not only
had skill, but originality and ingenuity. Their
pottery is varied in form and attractive in its or-
namentation. They understood how to plan
great architectural and engineering works and
to carry them to a satisfactory conclusion.

The soil of the terraces is extremely fer-
tile, and the Incas utilized every square yard of
available land within a radius of several miles.
The two or three Indian families who have been
living at Machu Picchu for the past four or five
years have had no difficulty in raising good

THE ALTAR OF THE CHIEF TEMPLE OF MACHU PICCHU

The interior of the Chief Temple on the Sacred Plaza, showing the cracking caused by the settling of the east wall. Notice the care with which the size of the stones is made to decrease gradually in each ascending tier. The main altar stone is 14 feet in length and a little over 5 feet in height.

A MASTERPIECE OF PREHISTORIC CONSTRUCTON

The east wall of the Chief Temple on the Sacred Plaza. The relative size of the large stone in the left-hand corner, which is 13½ feet in length and nearly 8 feet in height, may be gathered better from the next picture.

86

Photo by Hiram Bingham

TYPICAL INDIAN WOMEN AT MACHU PICCHU

The largest stone in the east wall of the Chief Temple on the Sacred Plaza and the wives of two workmen.

Photo by Hiram Bingham

THE HEAVIEST STONE BLOCK IN A MACHU PICCHU WALL

The interior face of the same stone and the ornamental niches in the east wall of the Chief Temple. The hole in the upper right-hand corner was undoubtedly for the admission of the beam which supported the roof of this temple.

Photo by Hiram Bingham

THE HIGH PRIEST'S HOUSE: MACHU PICCHU

This picture of the interior of the priest's house gives a better idea of the stone of the 32 angles. Not only were portions of two niches cut out of this stone, but in a spirit of freakish ingenuity the builders carried a small portion of the stone around the corner, so that a part of the corner itself is in this extraordinary block.

Photo by Hiram Bingham

THE HIGH PRIEST'S COUCH

Another view of the interior of the priest's house, showing the long bench, or platform, which was probably used as a couch. Notice the care with which the stones were selected, cut, and symmetrically arranged.

Photo by Hiram Bingham

THE SACRED PLAZA: MACHU PICCHU

This general view of the Sacred Plaza was taken at the conclusion of the season's work after the excavations had been finished and the ground releveled; showing the efforts that were made to leave everything in as good, if not better, condition than when we found it. The structure at the right, built in an entirely different style from the others, was probably originally covered with stucco, so that the general appearance of this plaza was anciently of a more symmetrical appearance than it is at present. In the floor of this building were found several bottle-shaped graves that had been opened many years previously. The structure at the left, the Chief Temple, is unquestionably one of the most remarkable architectural achievements of the Incas. In the center are ruins of what we have called the Temple of the Three Windows. As the windows are far too large for comfort in this cold climate, and are placed in a most conspicuous position, the conclusion reached is that they were symbolical. We believe they are connected with the tradition of the origin of the Incas.

Photo by Hiram Bingham

INTIHUATANA HILL AND THE TERRACES WEST OF THE SACRED PLAZA

On the left may be seen some of the precipices which defended Machu Picchu from attack. In the foreground are a group of the terraces where the ancient inhabitants raised their crops. Rising above these is Intihuatana Hill, crowned by its little temple. Just to the left of the temple may be seen the Sun Dial Rock. To the right of the hill is the Chief Temple and the Sacred Plaza. By comparing this with the view on page 94, the effects of the clearing in 1912 are brought out very clearly.

THE SUN DIAL: MACHU PICCHU

On top of the sacred hill is a curiously carved stone called an *Intihuatana* stone, or sun dial, or sun circle. *"Inti"* means "sun," and *"huatana"* a "rope," in Quichua, the language of the Incas. *Intihuatana* stones are found also in Cuzco and in Pisac and Ollantaytambo.

A GEM OF INCA ARCHITECTURE

The little temple on top of the sacred hill near the Intihuatana stone.

90

THE ARCHITECTURAL CENTER OF MACHU PICCHU

Apart from the Sacred Plaza, this is the center of the finest stonework in Machu Picchu. On the right is the beautiful outer wall of the group that is characterized by having the steepest gables and the finest monolithic lintels. In the center is a portion of the longest stairway, the one in which fountains are introduced at various stages. On the extreme left is a portion of the semicircular tower and the window of the snakes.

THE AGRICULTURAL TERRACES WHERE THE ANCIENT INHABITANTS OF
MACHU PICCHU RAISED THEIR CROPS

High up on the right may be seen part of the Upper City and the buildings of the Princess Group. Just beyond these is the inner city wall and the dry moat, which comes down the hill just outside the building in the lower center of the picture. Above this, in the center of the terraces, may be seen the archeological camp, and to the left the group called the *outer barracks*, outside of which runs the outer wall of the defenses of Machu Picchu. On the slopes in the distance are the ruins of ancient terraces that have been carried away by recent landslides. Every available foot of the country was once under cultivation.

Photo by Hiram Bingham

THE WESTERN PRECIPICES: MACHU PICCHU

Forest trees growing wherever there is a foothold have usually been found in this region to cover ancient agricultural terraces, and they probably do in the cases shown in this picture. The western trail to Machu Picchu climbs out of the cañon in the lower right-hand corner and winds up the precipice until it passes over the shoulder near the top of the precipice.

Photo by Hiram Bingham

A DISTANT VIEW OF OUR FIRST CAMP: MACHU PICCHU

A view looking over the tops of two of the houses of Ingenuity Group toward our camp and some of the agricultural terraces. The beams on top of one of the houses were placed there recently by one of our Indians, who thought this might make a good modern dwelling, but he found it too large for comfort. The huts of the modern Indians are much smaller than these houses and have no windows. It is possible that this may indicate that the climate has grown colder as well as dryer.

Photo by Hiram Bingham

THE WEST SIDE OF MACHU PICCHU

General view of Machu Picchu, showing (reading from right to left) the sacred hill, the Temple of the Three Windows and the Sacred Plaza, the principal cross street in the city and one of the finest stairways, a group of houses characterized by having four doors in the principal house, the beautiful outer wall of the King's Group, and finally the semicircular tower of the Princess Group.

Photo by Hiram Bingham

THE NORTH SIDE OF MACHU PICCHU

General view of the north and east side of Machu Picchu, showing (reading from left to right) the Sacred Plaza, the sacred hill, the inner garden terraces, the peak called Huayna Picchu, the Private Garden Group, and a carved stone which commands a magnificent view of the Urubamba Cañon. A comparison of this picture with that on page 89 shows the tremendous work of clearing that the expedition accomplished.

crops of sweet potatoes, corn, peppers, onions, tomatoes, and certain native vegetables unknown in this country. The only difficulty they have found is in keeping down the superabundant tropical vegetation, which constantly threatens to suffocate their crops.

As an instance of how rapidly this vegetation grows, terraces covered by bamboo cane which we cleared in September had to be recleared in November, when most of these pictures were taken. In the intervening two months some of the cane had attained a height of five feet.

It is my hope to prepare a special monograph on Machu Picchu for publication by the National Geographic Society.

II
DISCOVERY OF THE "CUZCO BONES" IN 1911

Another discovery made in 1911 was of the so-called Cuzco bones. The age of certain human and other bones found interstratified with glacial gravel near Cuzco was provisionally estimated by Prof. Isaiah Bowman, the geologist of the 1911 expedition, as from 20,000 to 40,000

Photo by E. C. Erdis

TIIE DIRECTOR AT REST: MACHU PICCHU CAMP

The main tent in the camp at Machu Picchu and the Director at the completion of the season's work.

years. These bones were brought to New Haven and submitted for examination to Dr. George F. Eaton, osteologist of the Peabody Museum.

In describing them in an article in the *American Journal of Science* for April, 1912, he says in his conclusion: "It is clear that no proof of great antiquity can be drawn from the characters of the human skeletal parts submitted to me, agreeing, as they do, in all essential respects with the bones of a recent people. Until additional skeletal material is obtained, showing characters more primitive than those already noted, the burden of proof of great antiquity must rest on geological and paleontological evidence."

Such geological evidence as we had been able to collect in the limited time at our disposal was presented by Professor Bowman in a paper published at the same time. Professor Bowman had reported several years before finding evidences of man's existence in the central Andes in late Glacial or early post-Glacial times. He was led to believe that the actual remains of man found in the Cuzco basin were embedded in gravels of a still earlier date.

DETERMINING THE AGE OF THESE BONES

In his interpretation of the geological and geographical evidence he reached the conclusion that the beds belonged to a Glacial series, and that the age of the vertebrate remains might be provisionally estimated at from 20 to 40 thousand years.

But he called attention to the weakness of the case, lying in the following facts: (1) that certain of the bones could not be sharply differentiated from those of modern cattle, and (2) that it was within the limits of possibility that the

Photo by Hiram Bingham

THE PLAZA OF SAYLLA: CUZCO VALLEY

In the Cuzco Valley, as well as on all the roads in the uplands of Peru, whenever an Indian passes through a village he stops to get a drink of *chicha*, the native beer, a large glass of which may be purchased for about two cents. When it is cleanly made, it is not disagreeable.

Photo by Hiram Bingham

A CORNER OF THE SAN FRANCISCO PLAZA: CUZCO

In the market-places of Cuzco and other Peruvian cities pottery made by the Indians in the vicinity is usually to be bought for prices ranging from five to fifty cents. It is hand made, baked in primitive ovens, and rudely decorated with variegated designs.

bluff in which the bones were found might be faced by younger gravel, and that therefore the bones had been in gravel veneer deposited during later periods of partial valley-filling.

He experienced grave doubts as to his own conclusions, because we were only able to spend a very few days in Cuzco after the find was made, and concluded his report with these words:

"Further excavation is needed, for the same body of gravels may yield material that will put the conclusions upon a more solid foundation. If later studies should yield evidence in favor of the conclusion that the material belongs to the Spanish period, we shall have still the fact of interstratification as a starting point, and the conclusions based upon that fact will have almost equal interest with the conclusions here stated, as to the Glacial age of the material. Changes of such magnitude indicate a swing of the climatic pendulum but little short of remarkable."

Since further examination of the Cuzco gravel beds and a comprehensive study of their age seemed essential, this was one of the chief objects of the 1912 expedition, and it was with this particular end in view that Professor Gregory and Dr. Eaton were asked to go to Cuzco.

IDENTIFYING THE "BISONIC" BONE

Among the bones Dr. Eaton had noted three fragments of bones belonging either to cattle or bison, whose specific identification was beset with almost insuperable difficulties. After examining skeletal bison remains in various museums and comparing them with these fragments and with similar bones of a number of North American domestic cattle, he found that one of the bones, a fragmentary bovine rib, was of a form which appeared to be characteristic of the bisons and different from the forms seen in North American domestic cattle.

Dr. Eaton had said in his published report: "It cannot be denied that the material examined suggests the possibility that some species of bison is here represented, yet it would hardly be in accordance with conservative methods to differentiate bison from domestic cattle solely by characters obtained from a study of the first ribs of a small number of individuals."

Consequently his first interest on reaching Cuzco was to secure specimen ribs of Cuzco domestic cattle. The very first one that we were able to procure from a local butcher shop told a new story.

Dr. Eaton reports as follows: "The plans for osteological work included the dissection of the carcasses of beef animals reared in the high altitudes of the province of Cuzco. This study revealed the fact that, under the life conditions prevailing in this part of the Andes, and possibly due to the increased action of the respiratory muscles in the rarefied air, domestic cattle can develop first ribs of 'bisonic' form.

There is, therefore, no reason for supposing that the bovine rib found with the human bones in the Ayahuaycco Quebrada in 1911 belongs to some species of bison, and any theory attributing great antiquity to the 'Cuzco man' based on such a supposition is untenable.

VALUABLE SPECIMENS EXCAVATED IN CUZCO VALLEY

"Systematic search in the Cuzco Valley for ethnological and paleontological material was carried on. Laborers were employed and excavations made in the terraces beneath the walls of the Sacsahuaman fortress; in the gardens of the Inca palace near the fortress and among the ruins of the near-by hill called Picchu. Several ancient graves on the hills overlooking the village of San Sebastian were explored. Much valuable material was collected, including human skeletons, belonging presumably to both the historic and prehistoric periods, together with the bones of contemporaneous lower animals, implements and ornaments of stone, bone, metal and shell, and pottery. The so-called 'ash deposits' of the city were examined, and specimens were obtained that will probably show that these deposits do not go back of the Hispanic period.

"Two days were spent making a reconnaissance of fossil beds near Ayusbamba [near Paruro], about 30 miles southwest from Cuzco, and the results of this brief visit gave such promise that later in the season another trip was made to this interesting locality in company with the geologist and two topographers. Although the locality had already been visited several times by amateur collecting parties, it was still possible to obtain a considerable amount of vertebrate material that will probably yield very satisfactory results."

Photo by Hiram Bingham

THE OSTEOLOGIST AT WORK: CUZCO VALLEY

In the north bank of the Huatanay River, a mile below Cuzco, Dr. Eaton found a human skeleton interstratified with clays and gravels 8 feet underground. Since the time when the bones were deposited there, the entire field of coarse gravels had been laid there above them, and in the succeeding centuries the river had cut down the bank until it finally laid them bare.

Photo by Hiram Bingham

A NEGLECTED SCIENTIFIC OPPORTUNITY: CUZCO VALLEY

Another view of the ruins at Tipon, near Oropesa. Recent unauthorized excavations by treasure hunters in this vicinity have brought to light important finds. This is one of the localities where careful systematic archeological excavation ought to be done in the near future. Although within a few miles of Cuzco, it has been visited by very few people.

GEOLOGICAL INVESTIGATIONS

The geological examination of the Cuzco Valley undertaken by Professor Gregory consisted, in the first place, of a study of the gravel deposits near Cuzco and the relation in age and position of these gravels to the remains of men and other animals discovered in them, both on the present and on the former expedition. In a preliminary summary of his investigations Professor Gregory says: "The gravels were found to be portions of an extensive alluvial fan of Glacial age, but the human relics embedded in them are probably of much later date." These deposits will be described fully in a paper on the Cuzco gravels to be published in the near future.

In regard to the other parts of his work, Professor Gregory reports as follows:

It consisted of "an examination of the structure, stratigraphy, and physiography of the Cuzco Valley with a view to securing the data for a geologic map of the area tributary to the Huatanay River. The region was found to consist chiefly of sedimentary rocks of pre-Tertiary, Tertiary, and Pleistocene age. Basic igneous intrusions are present and five intrusive masses of andesite (?) are represented by outcrops. During Glacial times a lake occupied the upper part of the valley. Fossils from Mesozoic and recent strata are sufficient to determine the relations of at least part of the formations. The results of the geologic survey, including stratigraphic and petrographic maps, are to be embodied in a report dealing with the area as a whole."

Professor Gregory also made a survey of Ayusbamba, on the Apurimac River, the locality from which fossil vertebrates were collected by Dr. Eaton. The strata at Ayusbamba are clays and sands deposited in an ancient lake perched high above the valley floors at an altitude of over 11,000 feet.

The Island of the Sun, in Lake Titicaca, Bolivia, was studied by both Professor Gregory and Assistant Topographer Heald, with reference to its coal deposits. A collection of carboniferous fossils was secured.

THE TROUBLES OF A CARTOGRAPHER

Owing to a most unfortunate misunderstanding, occasioned by the difficulty of getting messages transmitted in an uninhabited region, quite a little of Mr. Bumstead's work was unintentionally destroyed. It was necessary for him to leave the Cuzco Basin and work on the Andine cross-section before the Cuzco map was completed. This was occasioned by the rapid approach of the rainy season. Arrangements were made with the chief engineer of the Southern railways to have the map photographed. The permanent contour lines were inked in, but all streams, roads, ruins, terraces, plane-table locations, and many geographical names and all elevations were left on the sheet in pencil.

The photographer thought that the map looked rather badly with all these pencil-marks on it, and a telegram was sent to the director, requesting permission to erase all pencil-marks. This telegram was received *six weeks* later, on my return from a difficult journey into the interior.

It was then too late to save Mr. Bumstead's work, for the photographer, impatient at the delay, and not receiving permission to clean the map, had gone ahead on his own responsibility and erased what a month of careful field-work could not replace. As Mr. Bumstead says in his report:

Photo by L. T. Nelson

A TYPICAL CUZCO INDIAN
MOTHER AND BABY

She is patiently holding the surgeon's yardstick and wondering why she was having her picture taken.

The new Peruvian government had stipulated in their decree that all the work of excavating *and exploring* must cease on the first of December, and the local authorities were directed to see to it that this order was carried out. In the limited time that remained it was impossible to finish the map of the Cuzco Valley as carefully as it had been begun.

It was decided, however, that it would be much better to map the area needed by the geologist as well as it could be done before the day set by the government for the conclusion of our work. Accordingly, great pains have been taken to show the true character of the topography.

Photo by L. T. Nelson

TYPICAL PERUVIAN MOUNTAIN INDIANS

Indian men at a railroad station not far from Cuzco, smiling at the Doctor's efforts to get the picture. As it was a cloudy day with rain threatening, the hat was worn wrong side up.

"... Only one who has seen his patient and painstaking work destroyed can imagine my feelings when I returned to Cuzco within about a week of the time when the new Peruvian government said we must stop all our work—weary and almost discouraged from a trip that had ended in profitless waiting in a leaky tent for a cold rain to stop and permit the work to proceed through a region where the rainy season had set in in good earnest—only to find that all the above mentioned penciling on the Cuzco Valley map had been completely and absolutely lost."

The scale of the Cuzco Valley map is 1 inch to the mile, and the contour interval is 100 feet. The map covers in all 174 square miles. It includes nearly all the territory that drains into the valley of the River Huatanay, which rises in the mountains back of Cuzco, flows through the city and under part of it between walls constructed by the Incas, crosses the bed of an ancient lake, and finally joins the upper waters of the Urubamba, called at this point the Vilcanota or Vilcamayu.

Peruvian rivers have a habit of changing their names every few miles, and this particular

Photo by Hiram Bingham

GOATHERDS AND SHEPHERDS: CUZCO VALLEY

The shepherds of the Cuzco Valley are usually small boys who, like David of old, spend their early years with slings in their hands tending their flocks.

ogy and osteology of this region. If extensive scientific archeological work is ever permitted in this region, this map will be of great service in determining the geographic influences in the location of the ruins.

III
MAP-WORK OF THE EXPEDITION

The map-work was under the direction of Mr. Albert H. Bumstead, for nine years a topographic engineer in the United States Geological Survey. Mr. Bumstead's work was seriously handicapped by the fact that the seasons seem to be changing in Peru, and an unexpectedly large amount of rain was encountered in

river is no exception. It is called at various times the Vilcanota, the Vilcamayu, the Rio Grande, the Urubamba, the Santa Ana, and finally unites with other rivers to form the Ucayali, one of the great branches of the Amazon.

Mr. Bumstead's map of Cuzco Valley shows the elevations and relative positions of Cuzco, the great cyclopean fortress of Sacsahuaman, and the four historic roads leading out of the ancient Inca capital. It also aims to bring out clearly the chief topographic and physiographic features that are characteristic of the locality. It will be used by Professor Gregory and Dr. Eaton as a basis for their reports on the geol-

what is technically known as the "dry season." Furthermore, the difficulties of making maps in a lofty plateau, where, for example, the bottom of the Cuzco Valley is more than twice as high as the top of Mount Washington, can hardly be appreciated except by those who have tried to do field-work at similar elevations.

In 1911, owing to lack of preliminary reconnaissance and excessively hard local conditions, the topographer of the expedition had been unable to do anything on the most difficult part of the cross-section map. This work was now undertaken by Chief Topographer Bumstead and Assistants Hardy and Little.

A route map was completed along a rarely used trail from Abancay, the capital of the department of Apurimac, across the Apurimac Valley via Pasaje to Lucma, this being the portion of the map not completed in 1911. Mr. Bumstead's map is on a scale of 1 inch to the mile, with a contour interval of 200 feet. It covers approximately 500 square miles. Frequent latitude and azimuth observations were made all along the route, and an occultation of a first-magnitude star was observed in connection with time sights on the moon and Jupiter immediately afterwards.

The route covered by this map is about 100 miles in length and passes through a great variety of very heavy mountainous country. The elevations here range from about 4,000 feet up to more than 19,000. The most important features represented on this map are the glaciers of that part of the Vilcabamba Cordillera between Choquetira, Arma, and Lucma. A large part of this country was under glaciation at no very distant date, and great pains were taken to bring out the glacial forms.

This map will be of great value in giving proper understanding of the physiography of the central Andes, and will be published in connection with Professor Bowman's account of the geological cross-section made in 1911.

In describing his work on this map, Mr. Bumstead says:

"With such meager control as time and bad weather permitted, I endeavored to make a map of as wide a strip of country as possible, that would first of all convey the same impression of the topography upon the person who should use the map as I had at the time that I made it; that is, I wanted my map to accurately describe the character of each mountain and valley shown. This I kept ever in mind, and frequently reached out five or six miles with estimated distances to sketch features as I saw them, knowing that even though their positions and elevations were far from right, the picture brought to mind by the use of the map would be far better than nothing at all.

"In the main, however, the map is fairly well controlled, and in the snow-and-glacier-covered mountains around Choquetira and Arma I took very great pains not only to show a good picture of this wonderful region, but to make an accurate and dependable topographic map as well, and I got good locations and elevations on all the peaks and many other points besides.

"In making this map we followed the route of Professor Bowman in 1911. He expected the work to be done in 21 days. I think it could have been done in 30 days of good weather, and done even better than I did it, though I took three months, as I was hampered by fog and rain and snow almost continually from the time we left Abancay. It was aggravating in the extreme to catch glimpses of the wonderful scenery as the clouds would lift or settle and then have the peaks disappear from view before they could be located and sketched."

It was hoped that Mr. Bumstead would be able to locate and get the elevation of Mount Salcantay while on this trip, but it remained cloudy during the entire time.

IV

THE LAST INCA CAPITAL—VITCOS

A map of the vicinity of the last Inca capital of Vitcos, including the present-day villages of Puquiura and Vilcabamba, was made on a scale of 3 inches = 1 mile, with 100-foot contours.

This country is of great interest to students of historical geography. It is in the midst of a wonderful labyrinth of tropical valleys and glacier-clad mountains. Readers of Prescott's "Conquest of Peru," a book whose charm is as fresh today as it ever was, will remember that Pizarro selected Manco, a son of a former Inca, as the most available figurehead in whose name the Spaniards could govern Peru. He was crowned Inca in 1534, but he had too much good red blood in his veins to submit to Spanish tutelage, so he escaped, raised an army of faithful Indians, besieged Cuzco unsuccessfully, retreated to Ollantaytambo, and thence made good his escape into the fastnesses of this Andean labyrinth.

He found it easy to defend himself in this practically impregnable region called Vilcabamba, and he was able occasionally to make raids on Spanish caravans bound from Cuzco to Lima. A large part of the road over which he must have passed in making these raids was mapped for the first time by Mr. Bumstead, and is included in the Andean cross-section map referred to above.

The young Inca Manco lived at a place called Vitcos for 10 years. Here he actually received and entertained Spanish refugees. One of these, a hot-headed fellow, fell out with the Inca over a game of bowls (some writers say it was chess), and in the quarrel that ensued the Inca was killed.

MAP MAKING IN THE APURIMAC VALLEY

Photo by Hiram Bingham

Chief Topographer Bumstead working at his plane table making the map between Abancay and Pasaje. The difficulties of map making in cañons, varying from 4,000 to 10,000 feet in depth, can scarcely be appreciated except by practical engineers.

Two of his sons ruled in turn in his stead, so that for 35 years the country about Vitcos was governed by the Incas, and was all that was left to them of their magnificent South American empire.

PREVIOUS SEARCHES FOR VITCOS

When the famous Peruvian geographer, Raimondi, visited this region about the middle of the 19th century, no one seems to have thought of telling him that there were any ruins hereabouts. He knew that the young Inca Manco had established himself somewhere in this region, and he also knew that interesting ruins had been found at Choqquequirau, and described by the French explorer, Sartiges, in the *Revue des Deux Mondes* in 1851, so Raimondi concluded that the ruins of Choqquequirau must be those of the last Inca's long-lost capital.

Raimondi's proofs of the coincidence of Choqquequirau and the Inca capital are very vague, but as long as the only ruins reported from this region were those of Choqquequirau, nearly all the Peruvian writers, including the eminent geographer, Paz-Soldan, fell in with the idea that this was the refuge of Manco.

The word "Choqquequirau" means "cradle of gold," and this lent color to the story in the ancient chronicles that the Inca Manco had carried with him from Cuzco great quantities of gold utensils for use in his new capital.

Personally I did not feel so sure that the case was proven. The ruins did not seem fine enough for the Inca's residence. Consequently I was very glad that it was possible in 1911 to carry an exploring expedition into the Vilcabamba Valley, and still more delighted when we found interesting ruins at a place called Rosaspata.

Near Rosaspata was an extraordinary monolith, called "Ñusta Espana." By reference to the Spanish chroniclers, we found that it was recorded that near Vitcos, the last Inca capital, was a temple of the Sun, in which was a white rock over a spring of water. Furthermore, that Vitcos was on top of a high mountain, from which a large part of the surrounding region could be seen, and, moreover, that in the palace of Vitcos the doors, both ordinary and principal, were of white marble, beautifully carved.

WHY THE ÑUSTA ESPANA IS THE KEY TO THE IDENTIFICATION OF VITCOS

All of these points of description fitted the Rosaspata locality. Within half a mile of Rosaspata are the ruins of an ancient building which might have been the temple of the Sun, and in which is found a huge white rock, overhanging a spring of water. The ruins of Rosaspata are on top of a conspicuously high hill, from which the view in all directions is fine.

Finally the ruins of Rosaspata, unlike those of Machu Picchu and Choqquequirau, are noticeable because there are two kinds of doors, ordinary and principal ones, and that the doorposts are made of stones carefully carved out of white granite. (Strictly speaking, there is no *marble* in this region.) Furthermore, the rock at Ñusta Espana bears in its carvings marks which indicate that at one time in the remote past it was unquestionably an object of veneration.

This evidence made me believe that at Ñusta Espana was the principal shrine of the ancient people in this entire region, and that the neighboring ruins of Rosaspata were in reality the ruins of Vitcos, the last Inca capital. An account of the discovery of these places and a

Photo by Hiram Bingham

THE RESULTS OF EXCAVATION AT ÑUSTA ESPANA

The seats near the spring at Ñusta Espana after excavation. They are cut out of large rocks, so that the platform on which they rest, the seats themselves, and the lower portion of the back are all part of the same rock.
Thus only three or four large rocks were used for the entire row of seats. The excavations here yielded no
results in the way of potsherds or artifacts.

statement of the proof on which we have based
our conclusions may be found in *Harper's Magazine* for October, 1912, and in more extended
form in the Proceedings of the American Anti-
quarian Society for April, 1912.

Returning to this location in August, 1912,
I drained the marshes that partly surround the
rock at Ñusta Espana and excavated as far as was
practicable. To our surprise and mortification
we were unable to find any artifacts whatever
and only a handful of rough potsherds. We did
uncover an interesting priestly throne containing nine seats. The results of excavation are
shown above.

V

INCA PLACE NAMES IN THE
VILCABAMBA REGION

A problem which particularly occupied my
attention was the identification of ancient Inca
place names referring to the Vilcabamba country and occurring in the Spanish chronicles, but
not appearing on any known maps.

Before leaving New Haven I had an index
prepared of all the places that are referred to in
the available chronicles. A copy of this list was
taken with me in the field wherever I went, and
owing to the courtesy of the managers of vari-

ous plantations and of local government officials, the most intelligent and reliable Indians were carefully questioned in regard to these places.

By this means it is believed that a considerable body of geographical nomenclature has been assembled, and it is hoped that in the future it may be possible to write a report that will elucidate and interpret some of the more difficult passages in the chronicles.

VI
EXPLORATION OF THE AOBAMBA VALLEY

As part of our plan to cover the area included between the Urubamba and Apurimac rivers, an archeological and topographical reconnaissance was made of the hitherto unexplored Aobamba Valley. Assistant Topographer Heald undertook to approach this problem from the mouth of the valley at the junction of the Aobamba and Urubamba rivers. He met with almost insuperable difficulties.

Although the work looked easy as far as we could see from the mouth of the valley, he found that 4 miles from the mouth, up the winding stream, the jungle was so dense as to be almost impassable. There was no trail and the trees were so large and the foliage so dense that observations were impossible even after the trail had been cut. During a hard afternoon's work in jungle of this kind, with four or five men aiding in making the path, they succeeded in advancing only one mile.

Reconnaissance work in this type of jungle is extremely discouraging and unprofitable. Furthermore, there are occasionally some dangers—as, for instance, the following from Mr. Heald's account of his reconnaissance:

"On the way back to camp one of the men had a narrow escape from a snake, being grasped and held by another of the peons just in time to prevent his stepping on it. It was a small, dust-colored snake, about 10 inches long, and on being examined was found to possess two small poison fangs far back in the jaw. The fangs differed from those of most poisonous snakes in that they slanted back very little, coming almost straight down to the lower jaw."

THREE NEW GROUPS OF RUINS REPORTED

There was little of archeological interest in the portion of the valley which Mr. Heald succeeded in reaching. Quite unexpectedly, however, I got into the upper reaches of the valley about ten days later and found some interesting ruins and had an unexpected adventure. It happened on this wise:

The largest and richest estate in the Urubamba Valley, Huadquiña, is owned by the Señora Carmen Vargas, who inherited from her father about 1,000 square miles of land lying between the Urubamba and Apurimac rivers. Some of the land is occupied by sugar plantations; other parts are given over to the raising of sheep and cattle, while a large portion is still tropical jungle. Señora Carmen has always received us most hospitably and done everything in her power to further our efforts.

Her son-in-law, Don Tomas Alvistur, an enthusiastic amateur archeologist, took a considerable amount of interest in our work and was quite delighted when he discovered that some of the Indians on the plantation knew of three localities where there were Inca ruins, so they said, that had not previously been visited by white men.

Photo by Hiram Bingham

TAMPU MACHAI: NEAR CUZCO

A two hours' ride from Cuzco are the ruins of Tampu Machai, near the ancient fortress of Pucara. There is a spring here whose waters contain remarkable mineral qualities. Around it the ancients built a fountain and the ruins seem to be those of a temple dedicated to the god of the spring. This is one of the places of the Cuzco Valley that most urgently demands scientific investigation and careful study.

Don Tomas invited me to accompany him on a visit to these three groups of ruins, but when the time came to go he found that business engagements made it impossible for him to do more than accompany me part of the way to the first group. He went to the trouble however, of securing three Indian guides and carriers and gave them orders to carry my small outfit whenever it was impossible for the pack-mule to be used, and to guide me safely to the three ruins and home again.

They did not greatly relish these orders, but as they were all feudal tenants, holding their land on condition of rendering a certain amount of personal service every year in lieu of rent, they were constrained to carry out the orders of their overlord.

After Don Tomas departed I was left to the tender mercies of the Indians and of my faithful muleteer, Luis. The Indians had told us that one could visit all three ruins and return the next day. This information, however, did not prevent me from putting in supplies for at least a five days' journey, although I little anticipated what was actually going to happen.

The end of the first day's journey found us on top of a ridge about 5,000 feet above the place where we had started, in the midst of a number of primitive ruins and two or three modern huts.

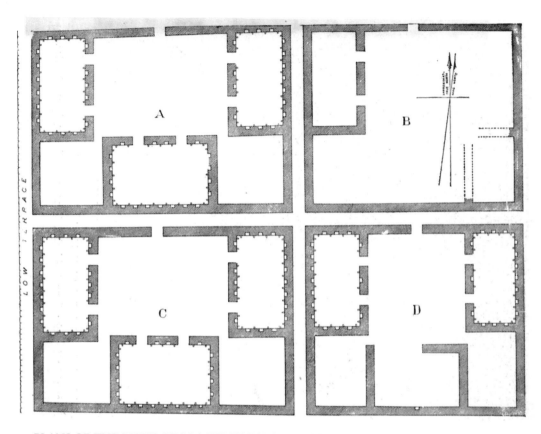

PLANS OF THE RUINS OF LLACTA IN PALCAY DISCOVERED IN 1912 (see text, next page)

The most remarkable feature of this fortified stronghold is that the cross-streets represent as nearly the exact cardinal points as it was possible for men working with crude tools to effect. These ruins are in the Southern Hemisphere, so the North Star is not visible. The ancient Peruvians did not know the use of the compass, and if they had the buildings would have been arranged according to the magnetic north and not according to true north. So exactly do the streets follow the local meridian and parallel that the exact orientation can hardly be said to be an accident.

LLACTA PATA, THE RUINS OF AN INCA CASTLE

This place was called Llacta Pata. We found evidence that some Inca chieftain had built his castle here and had included in the plan ten or a dozen buildings. They are made of rough stones laid in mud, with the usual sym-metrical arrangement of doors and niches. It would be interesting to excavate here for three or four weeks and get sufficient evidence in the way of sherds and artifacts to show just what connection the people who built and occupied this mountain stronghold had to the other occupants of the valley.

After measuring the ruins and taking a few photographs, I asked the Indians how far it was to the next group of ruins, and was told it was "two or three hours' journey."

Possibly it *could* be done by an Indian runner, with nothing to carry, in four or five hours, but we had three mules, that is, our two saddle-mules and the one pack-mule, whose load, weighing about 100 pounds, included a small tent, cooking outfit, blankets, and enough provisions for five days.

Although I had selected for this journey one of the best and strongest pack-mules which we possessed, and although his load was not much more than a third of what he could comfortably carry on a good road, he found it impossible to carry this load over the trail that we found before us.

During the first two or three hours the trail passed through a dense tropical jungle. We repeatedly had to make detours to avoid deep sloughs, and occasionally had to stop in order to have branches cut away so that the mules might get through.

DIFFICULT GOING

The trail grew rapidly worse, the pack-mule fell down four or five times, and finally became so frightened that he refused to attempt a place in the trail where it was necessary for him to jump up about four feet on a slippery rock. It was consequently necessary to unload him and distribute the cargo among the Indian carriers, and get all hands to help pull and push the mules over the bad spots in the mountain foot trail. This went on at intervals during the remainder of the day.

As a result we found ourselves at nightfall on a grassy slope on the side of the mountain about 15,000 feet above sea-level. A little shelter here and the presence of a small spring made the Indians prefer to pass the night at this point.

The next morning we crossed a high pass and descended rapidly into a steep-walled valley, containing one of the upper tributaries of the Aobamba. The lower slopes were covered with a dense forest, which gradually gave way to scrub and grass up to the snow-line. About 2 o'clock in the afternoon we reached the valley bottom at a point where several smaller tributaries unite to form the principal west branch of the Aobamba. The place was called Palcay.

Here we found two or three modern Indian huts, one of them located in a very interesting ruined stronghold called Llacta. As the location of the stronghold in the bottom of a valley was not easily defensible, a wall about 12 feet in height surrounded the quadrangular ruin.

The stronghold was about 145 feet square and divided by two narrow cross-streets into four equal quarters. Two of these quarters had been completed, and consisted of five houses arranged around a courtyard in a symmetrical fashion. The third quarter was almost complete, while the fourth quarter had only the beginnings of two or three houses. Each one of the four quarters had a single entrance gate on its north side. This will be more readily understood by consulting the plan.

The characteristics of the buildings are distinctly Inca and resemble in many ways those found at Choqquequirau in 1909. The stronghold was made of blocks of stone laid in mud, the buildings of symmetrical pattern, with doors narrower at the top than at the bottom; no windows, but interior ornaments of niches and projecting cylinders alternating between the niches. Whenever the wind did not blow, the gnats were very bad, which made the work of measuring and mapping the ruins extremely annoying.

DESERTED BY THE INDIAN GUIDES

I should like to have continued the journey the next day, but the Indians objected, saying that it was Sunday and that they needed the rest. This "rest" gave them an opportunity for concocting a plan of escape, and on Monday morning, when I was ready to start for the third group of ruins, there were no guides or carriers in sight.

Neither Luis nor I had ever been in the region before. We could of course have gone back on foot over the trail on which we had come, but it was very doubtful whether we could have succeeded in getting our mules over that trail, even though we had abandoned our outfit, and we knew that a loaded mule could not possibly go over the trail without constant assistance and a number of helping hands.

To aid us in our dilemma there came a little Indian who inhabited one of the huts near the ruins. He offered for a consideration to guide us out of the valley by another road, and said

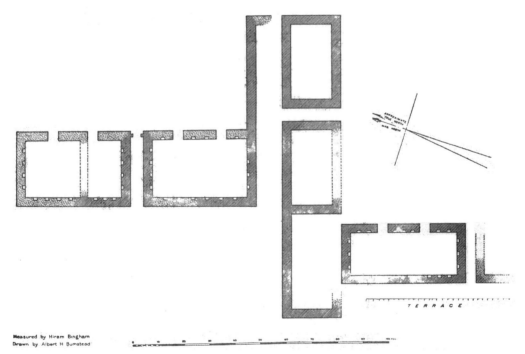

Measured by Hiram Bingham
Drawn by Albert H Bumstead

PLAN OF THE RUINS OF LLACTA PATA NEAR HUADQUIÑA,
DISCOVERED BY HIRAM BINGHAM IN 1912 (see text, page 109)

This plan shows the more important group of ruins at Llacta Pata. As in all Inca ruins, the marked characteristic is the symmetrical arrangement of niches within oblong buildings.

that it went near the other ruins. He also said that it might not be possible to use this road "if the pass had much snow in it."

We talked to him with difficulty, for, like most mountain Indians, he had no knowledge of Spanish, and our own knowledge of Quichua was somewhat limited. However, there was nothing for it but to follow our new guide, and by distributing the cargo on the three mules make it as easy as possible for the poor beasts to use the foot-path, or goat trail, which was indicated as our "road."

We had not gone more than half a mile before an abrupt ascent in the trail and a huge sloping rock barred the way for the mules for over half an hour. This difficulty being surmounted, we went on for another mile, only to find our way crossed by a huge avalanche of gigantic granite boulders and glacial drift, which had come down from the slopes of Mount Salcantay during the past year. A couple of hours were spent in negotiating the trail across this landslide.

We then found ourselves near the ruins of a village. Judging by the primitive appearance of the ruins, it could not have been a place of much importance and it is impossible to say whether it had been occupied since the Spanish conquest or not.

THE DISCOVERY
OF TEN MAGNIFICENT GLACIERS

Climbing up the valley beyond this ruined village and turning a corner, we came into full view of 10 magnificent glaciers—eight of them in a cirque in front of us and two on the slopes of Salcantay behind us. As the guide was very well informed as to the names of different parts of the valley and could give names for most of the peaks but none for any for the glaciers, I have named these as follows:

(1) *Hadley Glacier*, in honor of the President of Yale University.

(2) *Gannett Glacier*, in honor of the President of the National Geographic Society.

(3) *Grosvenor Glacier*, in honor of the Editor and Director of the National Geographic Society.

(4) *Bryce Glacier*, in honor of His Excellency James Bryce, the British Ambassador, whose interest and enthusiastic support has greatly stimulated our work.

(5) *Harkness Glacier*, in honor of Edward S. Harkness, Esq., of New York, whose generous assistance was largely responsible for making possible the expeditions of 1911 and 1912.

(6) *Alfreda Mitchell Glacier*, in honor of my wife, without whose cooperation none of this work could have been done.

(7) *Taft Glacier*, in recognition of the courteous assistance we received from the United States government.

(8) *Leguia Glacier*, in recognition of the courteous assistance we received from the Peruvian government.

(9) *Morkill Glacier*, in recognition of the courteous assistance we received from the Peruvian corporation.

(10) *Yale Glacier*—for obvious reasons.

While we were enjoying the wonderful spectacle and wondering whether any civilized being had ever seen the glaciers before, a magnificent gray deer with eight prongs to his horns sprang out of the grass near us, gave us a long look of interested interrogation, and then dashed off to find his friends.

Our little guide was more interested in the looks of the pass than in the deer, and although he shook his head as it came into view, it seemed

Photo by Hiram Bingham

THE FINEST STONEWORK AT RUMI CCOLCA: CUZCO VALLEY

A detail of one side of the gateway at Rumi Ccolca, which shows stone blocks cut with as much precision as the best work at Machu Picchu. The projecting nubbins left on these rocks are an echo of similar marks left on the stone inside the priest's house near the Sacred Plaza in Machu Picchu.

to us that we were most fortunate, for there appeared to be no snow whatever on the trail all the way to the top of the pass. But we neglected to take into account the fact that we were approaching the pass from the north or sunny side, and that there might be snow on the trail on the other side of the pass, on the south or shady slope.

THE GRANDEUR OF THE SCENERY

All thoughts of this, however, were temporarily swept aside by the magnificent view of Salcantay, which we now had on our right hand.

In many ways it is an ideally beautiful peak, rising as it does to a sharp point, with its sides covered with snow and ice, and lifting its head so magnificently thousands of feet higher than anything else in the vicinity.

Our own elevation at the time was a little over 16,000 feet, and a conservative estimate would place the top of the mountain at least 5,000 feet above us. It was a very great disappointment that we were unable, owing to the bad weather, to get the mountain triangulated, so that its height still remains an unknown quantity.

The American mining engineers at Ferrobamba believe it to be the highest peak in the Andes, and Mr. Stevens, the superintendent of the mine, which is nearly 100 miles away from the mountain, told me that he had seen it from so many distant points of the Andes that he felt confident it must be the highest mountain in South America.

Just before getting to the top of the pass we turned aside for a few moments to see the remains of a hole in the ground where it is said that there was once an ancient gold mine.

A few specimens of rock brought from the talings appear to contain small quantities of silver and copper, but the altitude is so great and the surroundings so difficult that it is not likely that this mine will ever be a profitable working proposition.

THE MULES STAMPEDE ON A SNOW SLOPE

Our joy in the scarcity of snow on the north side of the pass was instantly reduced to despair when we reached the summit and looked down a precipitous slope covered with snow for a distance of at least 1,000 feet below us.

The sandal-shod mountain Indians, whose occasional huts are the only signs of human habitation hereabouts, had made a zig-zag path in the snow by means of tramping down the upper crust with roughly cut stumps of stunted mountain trees. The path was about eight inches wide.

Our mules had never been in the snow before. At first our Indian guide declared he would not go down with us, as he was afraid of snow blindness, but he was persuaded to accompany us.

Our mules took a few steps on the little path, then decided that the white snow field looked more inviting and left the path, fell into the soft snow up to their ears, floundered around and attempted to stampede, and rolled down the side of the mountain. It was nearly half an hour before we got them safely back on the trail again, where they stood trembling and unwilling to attempt the descent. Coaxing and curses were equally of no avail. Pulling, hauling, and beating were alternately resorted to.

Somehow or other, chiefly because our trail lay down hill, so that when they fell and floundered off the path they always landed a little nearer to their goal than when they had started, we eventually got the mules to the foot of the declivity, but only after several narrow escapes and three hours of hard work. As we looked back up the trail it seemed that perhaps 1,500 feet would be a more exact estimate of the height of the snow-covered slope.

Just at dusk we reached the first hut in the valley, and found that we were in one of the upper branches of the Chamaná River, a tributary of the Urubamba, which Mr. Tucker, of the 1911 expedition, had reconnoitered the preceding year.

DISCOVERY OF THE PICTOGRAPHIC ROCK

In this valley was the third group of ruins which we had been told about. Their most unusual feature lay in the fact that the Incas, desiring to save as much of the upland valley floor as possible for agricultural purposes, had straightened the bed of the meandering stream and inclosed it in a stone-lined channel, making it practically perfectly straight for nearly three-quarters of a mile.

The valley is still used to a certain extent for raising and freezing potatoes. The owner of the hut near which we camped entertained our Indian guide in compensation for his assistance in spreading potatoes to be frozen that night some distance below us in the valley bottom. The next day our guide took us back up the valley and out through a smaller tributary, where we crossed the divide between the Urubamba and Apurimac valleys and descended toward the town of Limatambo.

This was one of the most fortunate accidents of the trip, for had we decided to go down the Chamaná over Mr. Tucker's route and return quickly down the Urubamba to our starting point, we should have missed seeing a most interesting rock which lay alongside of the little path we followed on this day's journey.

Neither the guide nor the muleteer had their eyes open for petroglyphic or pictographic markings, and so did not notice that they had passed close to the only rock so far discovered in the department of Cuzco that contains petroglyphs. Others have been reported by vague rumor, but none so far have been located except this one, whose existence was known to one or two cowboys on a neighboring ranch.

The character of the petroglyphs is essentially savage. They remind one of some of the glyphs used by our own western Indians. It seems to me possible that these marks were left on this rock by an Amazon Indian tribe who came thus far on the road to Cuzco. In the vicinity there were a few groups of stones which might indicate the former presence of rude huts, but until a comparative study can be made of all the pictographs and petroglyphs in Peru and in the Amazon basin it will be difficult to speak very definitely about this new discovery.

That night I was most hospitably entertained at a small ranch house and the next day made a forced march to Cuzco, reaching there shortly before midnight. This journey, which began so inauspiciously and might have ended in disastrous failure, actually produced more results in the discovery of hitherto undescribed ruins than any other part of the work.

VII
CHOQQUEQUIRAU

In 1909, owing to the courtesy of the Peruvian government and at their urgent invitation, I had visited the ruins of Choqquequirau. An account of this visit was published in the *American Anthropologist* for October-December, 1910 (pages 505-525), and also in my *Across South America*, pages 291-323.

A French expedition had visited the ruins about 60 years before and had reached them from the north, over a path that has turned back several expeditions since then. In 1909, owing to the existence of a small temporary bridge, I was able to reach them from the south, but had not found it possible to spend more than four days there.

That bridge disappeared some time ago, and as it was now deemed advisable to attempt a further reconnaissance of those celebrated ruins, I asked Mr. Heald to see whether he could not reach them from the north, across the cordillera of Vilcabamba. An enthusiastic young German merchant in Cuzco had attempted this feat two years before, but failed to get more than half way from Yanama, the nearest settlement.

Knowing Mr. Heald's pluck, I felt sure that he could get there if anybody could, but that if he failed the only alternative must be to reconstruct the bridge over the Apurimac. The latter would have been a serious undertaking, as the river is over 200 feet wide and the rapids are strong and very dangerous.

Mr. Heald not only succeeded in reaching Choqquequirau, but visited the place three times, made a passable trail, and was able to conduct thither Dr. Eaton and Dr. Nelson. Their stay was limited by the very great difficulties which they encountered in securing laborers to accompany them, and in carrying sufficient food for themselves and the laborers over the extremely rough country.

A HARD DAY'S WORK

As a sample of the difficulties encountered, let me quote the following from Mr. Heald's account of his first day out from Yanama:

"... After a three hours' climb we reached a spot well above 14,000 feet and had a splendid view of the country. From here I could get an idea of the kind of traveling I would encounter, and it did not look very inviting. Where the jungle was not thick the mountain-sides were steep and rocky. I could see the course of the Apurimac, somewhere near which was Choqquequirau, and the green cane fields in the province of Abancay, on the other side.

"From a purely artistic point of view the country was wonderful, with its splendid ranges of gleaming white peaks all covered by glaciers, and the dark green of the jungle below leading down into straight-sided valleys with streams white with foam running down them. From the point of view of one who had to travel through it for the purpose of getting to a place, location unknown, and making a trail to that place, it was anything but lovely. . . .

"After looking my fill and taking compass readings on Yanama and various prominent

points, we started down. There had been condors swinging above us ever since we had reached the high point, and now one flew quite close. I fired at him with the 22 Winchester automatic, and for a moment thought he was going to fall. He recovered his balance, however, and went sailing off; but after traveling about half a mile he suddenly collapsed and fell, turning over and over and over into the brush, where, after quite a hunt, we found him, dead.

"He was a splendid bird, spreading a little over 9 feet 6 inches and measuring 4 feet from bill to tail tip. This shot showed both the hitting power of the little 22 and the wonderful vitality of the condor. The mushroom bullet had gone through breast and breast-bone, lungs, liver, and intestines, lodging against a thigh-bone. Tomás carried the bird back to the hacienda, where the prowess of the little rifle caused much admiration. We took off the skin and spread it to dry on one of the frames built to jerk meat, of which there were several in the yard. Next morning it was nowhere to be seen, and, as the mayor-domo said that it was no use looking for it, I surmised that he knew where it was and agreed with him. . . ."

TROUBLE WITH BEARS
AND JUNGLE FLIES

Dr. Eaton's party had some trouble with hungry bears, which broke open a food box and devoured a quantity of precious provisions. These bears belong to the *spectacled-bear* genus, and, although plentiful in this region, are extremely shy and hard to get a shot at.

The perils of the trail were many, but the most serious handicap, as every explorer has found in this region before, and the most an-

Photo by Hiram Bingham

THE SACRED WHITE ROCK NEAR VITCOS

A general view of the great monolith at Ñusta Espana, near Puquiura. Part of the rock overhangs a spring of water. This shrine is described in the early chronicles of Augustinian missionaries. Near here was Vitcos, the last Inca capital.

noying thing they had to endure, was the ever-present swarms of green jungle-flies. Mr. Heald says in his report:

"They are little fellows, but the way they bite is not the least in proportion to their size. Every place they bite they leave a blood-spot the size of a pin-head, and this burns and itches for two or three days. There were swarms of them, and soon we were all swelling. The only thing we could do was to grin and bear it. When we stopped to rest we made a smudge, but while traveling the best we could do was to slaughter as many as we could.

"... With the coming of dark the flies had left us, but they left us in very bad shape. Not a man of us could bend his wrists, they were so swollen; the knuckles on the hands were invisible, and our eyes were mere slits that it cost an effort to open enough to look out of. Still, there was a lot to be thankful for. There was lots of dry wood where we stopped, and we soon had a fire going, which warmed and dried us. The night was clear, so there was no danger of being gotten out of bed by rain. I had shot a jungle duck, and the inner man was perfectly satisfied. What bothered me most was that I was afraid the peons would try to run away, and I very much doubted my ability to carry enough food to enable us to find Choqquequirau without their help. . . ."

THE SCARCITY OF WATER AND SUFFERING FROM THIRST

Their most serious difficulty, however, was the lack of water and the height and steepness of the mountains, which cut them off from any possible water supply. Here is a sample of what they suffered:

"The next morning, when I went to fill my canteen with water, I found that there was none. The men said that they had drunk it, but I felt pretty sure that they had poured it out, believing that then we would have to turn back. I would have done so (though no farther than the spring we had uncovered the day before), but the Director had told me there was a spring easily found at Choqquequirau, and I was confident that we must be near the place.

"In front of us rose a sharp ridge. I was sure that if we gained its top we would see the city on the other side. The fire had cleared the ground, so going was not hard; it had also cleared out the flies. After about two hours of climbing we stood on top of the lowest saddle of the ridge. This had been reached after some rather ticklish cliff-climbing. On looking over the other side we were tremendously disappointed, for instead of a city there was an impassable ravine. All the morning we worked along the knife edge of ravines, hoping that the city would come into view, and always disappointed.

"By noon we had come to where the ridge merged into the mountain proper and were working along its sides. After the stop for lunch the men refused to go any farther. They said if they did it would be merely to die of thirst; that the city of Choqquequirau was non-existent, and that they did not wish to die just because I did.

EXTREME MEASURES BECOME NECESSARY

"I knew we couldn't make them work, but I thought we could force them to travel. Giving the 22 to Tomás, I told him to shoot any man who tried to bolt, but to do it carefully, around the edges. Then, taking a machete, I started ahead, cutting the way, and told them to follow. As Tomás stood between them and the back trail, they decided to do so, and for two hours we went ahead in that way. By that time I was just about exhausted, as we were working through thick cane and I was going at top speed.*

"Coming out on a little shoulder, I thought I saw some ruins on the next spur ahead. Looking through my glass confirmed it. Then I pointed them out to the men. They too saw them, and after that there was no trouble. They were as anxious to get there as I was, for we were all suffering from thirst, and I had told them there was a spring there.

"Two hours of hard work placed us on the spur, though still high above the ruins. From there we could see several stone houses and two thatched huts, which had been left by the treasure-hunters who had come from Abancay two years previously. Just at dark we reached these huts. They showed signs of the old occupancy. There were two or three skulls lying around. A table-stone or two were in evidence and in one corner was an old Inca pot.

". . . While four of us were fixing camp I sent the other two out to look for water. In an hour they came back with the news that there

* It should not be forgotten that all this time Mr. Heald was suffering from the effects of his accident on Huayna Picchu, which had partially disabled his right arm.

THE CURIOUS ROCKS OF CONCACHA

Photo by Hiram Bingham

Near Abancay, where the topographical cross-section of the Andes was begun in 1912, are some extraordinary carved rocks at a place called Concacha. This one is called by the Indians Rumihuasi, or stone house. It has been inadequately described by several travelers and the vicinity is one that demands early systematic investigation.

was none to be found. By this time we were all very thirsty, but there was nothing to do but grin and bear it.

WATER HARD TO FIND

"About midnight I was wakened by a man crying and pleading. It was Tomás, who was having a nightmare. This in itself would not have been serious, but it excited the superstitions of the peons. They said the Incas were angry because we were there, and they wanted to be gone at daylight. I thought it best to spend some time making a search for the

spring; so, as soon as it was light, we started and for an hour hunted in the jungle, but without result. The best we could do was to get water from air plants and chew certain bulbs which contained much moisture. This was not such a small help as it might seem, for many of the air plants had a good swallow of water in them, though of course we got it drop by drop at a time.

"Giving up hopes of finding a spring near the city, we took the back trail. We were all pretty weak, but we made very fair time. Reaching the ridge, we climbed down by a new way, marking our trail with piles of stones, and also followed a new trail back to the draw in which the spring was, striking the draw a good deal higher up. This turned out to be a better road; also it led us to the discovery of a series of stone-faced terraces, and at one point in them the spring broke through, so that with a little fixing we could get all the water we wanted, and that was a good deal."

They later found water within an hour's walk of Choqquequirau, and had a plentiful supply for the work of excavating as long as their provisions lasted.

They had hoped to accomplish a good deal of map-work, but, owing to the great amount of rain and the almost continuous prevalence of fog and mist, little could be done besides making a route map.

ACCIDENTS AMONG THE INDIANS

The Indians suffered quite as much as the white men on this journey. One of the bearers, who was carrying a food-box weighing 60 pounds, slipped on a steep bank and fell 20 feet; the box, which fell with him, opened his head. The man was not killed, but of course had to be sent home, and as laborers were extremely scarce, his presence was seriously missed.

Another Indian ran a stick into his foot and blood-poisoning ensued. A third slipped off a precipitous rock and fortunately was saved by the rope which had been tied to his waist when passing this dangerous part of the trail, although he had a toe-nail torn off and suffered considerably from blood-poisoning.

The results of these hardships were the route map—the first ever made of this section of the Andes—the discovery of a number of hitherto unknown Inca engineering works, including ditches and agricultural terraces, now

buried deep in the jungle and practically inaccessible, and a few boxes of archeological and osteological specimens.

Because of the scarcity of labor, the terror of the Indians, and the small quantity of provisions that could be carried over the extremely difficult trail, the party was only able to spend five days at Choqquequirau. Under Dr. Eaton's direction 11 graves were examined and such skeletal material and pottery collected as four men could carry on their return march. No metal objects were found in these graves.

The method of burial was similar to that observed at Machu Picchu, except that the construction of bottle-necked graves was far superior at Choqquequirau, and this style of grave apparently more in vogue than at Machu Picchu. It may be noted here as significant that apparently the best example of the bottle-necked grave at Machu Picchu was found in a house closely resembling in its architectural details the buildings at Choqquequirau.

This route had only been used three times previously: (1) by the French explorer Sartiges in 1834, (2) by the Peruvian explorer Samanez in 1861, and (3) by the Almanza brothers in 1885. It was used successfully this year for the first time since 1885. Great credit is due Mr. Heald for his courage and perseverance.

VIII
ANTHROPOLOGICAL STUDIES

The anthropological study consisted chiefly in the taking, with extreme care and marked regard for scientific accuracy, of a number of anthropometric measurements.

The blanks used for the measurements were prepared by Dr. H. B. Ferris, of the Yale Medical School, and the results and photo-

Photo by L. T. Nelson

"THE FATHER OF HIS COUNTRY"

About 150 Indian men were measured and photographed in an effort to get accurate information regarding their physiognomy and anatomy. Most of them were rather frightened, but this one, who has been dubbed the "father of his country," was very much flattered and highly pleased at having his picture taken.

graphs have been turned over to him for the preparation of a report on the anatomical char-

acteristics of the Mountain Indians of Southern Peru as represented in the data obtained by the expedition.

Owing to the habit that the Mountain Indians have of frequently visiting Cuzco, the principal center of population, we were enabled to secure measurements of representatives of many villages and towns that we did not visit. Besides Cuzco, anthropological measurements were taken in Huadquiña, Machu Picchu, and Santa Ana.

At Machu Picchu we had our own workmen to draw on, while at Santa Ana and Huadquiña the managers of the large sugar plantations kindly placed their laborers at our disposal. In Cuzco it was necessary to employ force. Had it not been for the willingness of the Peruvian government to assist us, we should have failed in our object.

The method followed was to have the officer or soldier who was assigned to us go out on the streets and arrest any Indians that seemed to be of pure blood and who proclaimed by their costumes and general appearance that they were typical Mountain Indians.

On being arrested, the unfortunate subjects were brought to the doctor's room at the hotel. Many of the Indians thought that they were being recruited for service in the army, and not a few shed tears at the thought; others were only curious. All were much relieved when they were set free and given a five-cent piece with which to buy *chicha* (native beer made from maize).

Thirty-eight measurements were taken of each subject—measurements of head, face, ears, and nose, as well as of height standing, kneeling, sitting, and others. Many other data were also recorded concerning any peculiarities or deformations, color of eyes and hair, and other facts of anthropological interest.

One hundred and forty-five Indians were thus studied, and a front and side view photograph taken of each. They represented 16 provinces and 60 towns. Most of these were men. Photographs of many Indian women were also taken in Cuzco and at the stations between Cuzco and Mollendo, making 433 photographs in all taken for this study.

Some of the Indians were greatly frightened at the procedure. To one aged Indian military honors appealed, and he took his measurements with a smiling face. Another Indian, when he found he could have his picture taken free, dressed in his Sunday clothes. The next day he returned to see the photograph. When he was shown the negative he refused to believe that it was his picture, because he couldn't see the colors and the spangles that decorated that Sunday coat he wore.

CONCLUSIONS REACHED FROM THE MEASUREMENTS AND EXAMINATIONS

At Huadquiña the Indians were ordered to a room to be measured. One subject objected strenuously and made it as difficult as he could for any measurements to be taken. He would not stand straight, nor sit straight, nor assume any position correctly. Finally, when the measurements were all taken, he was offered the usual *medio* for his trouble. This small coin, with which one could purchase a large drink of native beer, was usually gratefully accepted as a *quid pro quo*, but in this case the Indian decided he had been grievously insulted, and he threw the coin violently to the ground and strode off in high dudgeon.

Remarkably few cranial deformations were found, these being all slightly acrocephalic. The

Photo by L. T. Nelson

A TYPICAL CUZCO GIRL

A pleasant-faced Cuzco Indian girl holding a yardstick to give an idea of her height, and wearing the regulation costume of the Peruvian Mountain Indian women. The hat is a flat pancake of straw lined on one side with red flannel, and on the other side with blue velveteen decorated with strips of gilt braid. It may be worn either side up, according to the weather.

following facts were noticed about the Indians: The leg and back muscles are markedly developed, while their arm muscles show very meager development; their work consists largely of carrying heavy loads upon their backs over mountain trails; the Indians do not become bald, and their hair seldom loses its pigment; their teeth are also remarkably well preserved, except on the sugar plantations, where they suck the sugar-cane and eat coarse brown sugar (*chancaca*).

An interesting custom which still prevails was observed as being practiced about two miles outside of Cuzco, as one goes north toward the Urubamba Valley. At a point in the road where one gets a last look at the city the Indians have a praying place.

THE INDIAN PRAYING PLACE ABOVE CUZCO

This road is one of the principal highways in Peru, and hundreds of Indians pass up and down going in and out of Cuzco daily. The view of Cuzco lying below in the green valley is truly a beautiful one, but it is something more than a sense of beauty that makes the Indians stop, and, with uncovered heads, some kneeling and some standing, offer a prayer as they look toward their Mecca.

It is noticeable that those who are on a journey going away from Cuzco pray for a longer time than those who are approaching the city. Possibly they fear the dangers of the roadside more than those of the city streets.

Another Indian custom which adds a picturesque touch to the roadsides between Cuzco and Machu Picchu is the presence of quaint signs indicating what is for sale in the Indian huts.

A small bunch of wheat or barley tied on the end of a pole and stuck out in front of the hut indicates that there is *chicha* (a native corn beer) for sale within. A bunch of flowers on the end of a pole also has the same significance.

A green wreath means that there is bread for sale, while a piece of white cloth or white paper waving in the breeze indicates that the wayfarer may here purchase *aguardiente*, a powerful white rum made of cane juice and containing a large percentage of raw alcohol.

It is sincerely to be regretted that more Indians could not have been measured, but as this work was entirely in charge of the surgeon of the expedition, Dr. L. T. Nelson, and as his first duty was to attend to the health of the members of the expedition, the anthropological measurements had to take second place. The exigencies of the work necessitated his spending a large part of his time where there was little opportunity for making anthropological measurements.

NO MEASUREMENTS PERMITTED IN AREQUIPA

In Arequipa he found that local sentiment prevented the government from assisting him. Arequipeños would resent any action compelling an Indian to submit to measurements, even though the subject were paid for his time. Furthermore, as practically the only pure-blooded Indians now in Arequipa are transients who come in for commercial purposes, driving their llama trains loaded with produce, the merchants of Arequipa would resent anything which might interfere with business. These difficulties made it impossible to secure any measurements in Arequipa.

On the trip to Choqquequirau, where the surgeon's presence was necessary, owing to the great risks of sending the members of the expedition over a dangerous mountain trail, it was necessary to cut the equipment down to any

Photo by Hiram Bingham

POTTERY FROM MACHU PICCHU

such surgical instruments as might be demanded, and it was not possible to take along any of the equipment for making anthropometric measurements.

Finally, owing to the presence of smallpox and an epidemic of typhoid in Arma, Puquiura, and the neighboring villages, the surgeon was obliged to stay with the topographical party all the time that they were working in that region.

Their work was greatly hindered by adverse weather conditions, and so much valuable time was lost.

The extent of the smallpox and typhoid fever epidemics prohibited the surgeon from carrying on anthropological work there, on account of the danger of bringing the contagion to the camp. To be sure, the white members of the expedition had been vaccinated, both for smallpox and typhoid, by our medical adviser, Dr. H. S. Arnold, of the Yale Medical School, before leaving this country; but it would have been wrong to have had them run unnecessary risks or to have subjected to the danger of contagion the muleteers, engineering assistants, and the other native members of the party who had not been so vaccinated.

IX
WEATHER OBSERVATIONS

From May 28, the day of our departure from Panama, until the arrival of the vessel off the town of Mollendo, on June 8, a full series of weather observations was taken daily at the hours of 8 a. m., 12 m., and 8 p. m. The data recorded cover the following phenomena: Air temperature (dry-bulb thermometer), temperature by wet-bulb thermometer, barometric pressure, clouds, precipitation, wind, sea, and surface temperature of the ocean.

On the return voyage from Mollendo to Panama a full series of weather observations was taken similar to that recorded when outward bound.

A complete series of weather observations was taken at Machu Picchu and during the cross-section map-making. Arrangements were made with Mr. Burt Collins, the manager of the Inca Mining Company, and with Mr. Claude Barber, of the Santa Lucia mine, to undertake the establishment of four meteorological stations at widely different elevations along the 71st meridian west of Greenwich. One will be at an elevation of nearly 14,000 feet, another at an elevation of about 6,000 feet, another on the edge of the Great Plains, and still another on the River Madre de Dios.

Self-registering barometers, thermometers, and rain gauges have been supplied for these sta-tions. Mercurial barometers and sling psy-chrometers have also been provided. Both Mr. Collins and Mr. Barber have agreed to look after the maintenance of the stations for a period of five years.

The instrumental equipment for these stations was in part a loan from the Harvard Observatory through the kindness of Prof. E. C. Pickering, and in part due to the generosity of Mrs. Alfred Mitchell, who placed at our disposal a special fund for the purchase of instruments.

The results of the work should prove most illuminating and ought to be of particular value in connection with the observations made some years ago by the Meteorological Department of the Harvard Astronomical Observatory at Arequipa.

X
COLLECTIONS MADE
BY THE EXPEDITION

Our collections have all safely reached New Haven. They consist in large part of the bones of the people who built and lived in Machu Picchu, of the potsherds, pots, and bronzes found there, and of the geological, osteological, and paleontological material collected in the vicinity of Cuzco, of geological specimens from other parts of Peru, and of 2,500 photographs taken with the 3A Special and No. 4 Panaram Kodaks.

In a broad geographical sense the results of Dr. Eaton's collecting is one of the most important and interesting features of the expedition. In the vicinity of Cuzco Dr. Eaton secured the skeletons of probably 20 individuals. At Machu Picchu more than 60 individuals were excavated, and at Choqquequirau ten.

With these ancient denizens of southern Peru were found a number of bronze metal objects, including pins, knives, forceps, and some very attractive pieces of pottery. Although Dr. Eaton was technically the osteologist of the expedition, his work lay in a variety of fields.

Invertebrate fossils were collected from the hills overlooking the town of Payta, Peru, and the site of an ancient cemetery at Pascasmayo was visited.

Vertebrate fossils were obtained from sedimentary gravels in the Huancaro Quebrada.

ACKNOWLEDGMENTS

Acknowledgments are due to the United States government for kind offices in connection with securing requisite privileges in Peru and for the loan, on the part of the Army, of a detached service chest, which enabled us to have the use of an abundant supply of medicines and of a complete set of surgical instruments:

To the Peruvian government for many favors and courtesies, including the free entry of all our equipment and supplies, the assignment to our party of members of the Army whenever necessary, and the permission to bring all of our collections to this country.

To Mr. W. L. Morkill and the other officials of the Peruvian corporation and the Southern Railway of Peru for many courtesies, including the free use of their railway and telegraph lines.

To the President and Faculty of the University of Cuzco, who aided us in numerous ways and whose many courtesies included not only hospitable entertainment at houses of the professors, but assistance in finding interesting points whose whereabouts was not generally known.

To Messrs. Cesar Lomellini & Co., of Cuzco, who for two years have acted as our agents and have placed at our disposal their excellent facilities for handling the difficult situations which arise in connection with the organization and administration of an exploring expedition, and all without charging us any commission or any rent, although we occupied a large room in their warehouses as our headquarters for many months.

To Messrs. W. R. Grace & Co., whose unique position in Peruvian commerce enable them to assist us in unnumbered ways, beginning with the procuring of our supplies and ending with the carrying home of some of our collections in their steamers, without charge for any of their services. It is not too much to say that the work of the last two years could not have been accomplished as it has been without the continual friendly offices of this company, whose enlightened policy in regard to assisting scientific endeavor might well serve as an example to other companies engaged in carrying on foreign trade.

In conclusion it gives me great pleasure to acknowledge a large debt of gratitude to the officials of Yale University and of the National Geographic Society for their sympathetic cooperation during both the preparation and the progress of the expedition.

To them and to the members of the expedition I should like to take this opportunity to express my own personal thanks for the loyal support which has been accorded me from the beginning. The end is not yet, for it will take many months of patient and laborious effort to bring out the ultimate scientific results of the Peruvian Expedition of 1912.

FURTHER READING

Hiram Bingham's accounts of Machu Picchu still remain the best source for further reading. See especially *Machu Picchu: Citadel of the Incas* (1930) and *Lost City of the Incas* (1948, 1965). See also John Hemming, *The Conquest of the Incas* (1970) and Loren McIntyre, *The Incredible Incas and Their Timeless Land* (1975).

INDEX

CONTRIBUTORS

General Editor FRED L. ISRAEL is an award-winning historian. He received the Scribe's Award from the American Bar Association for his work on the Chelsea House series *The Justices of the United States Supreme Court.* A specialist in American history, he was general editor for Chelsea's *1897 Sears Roebuck Catalog.* Dr. Israel has also worked in association with Arthur M. Schlesinger, jr. on many projects, including *The History of the U.S. Presidential Elections* and *The History of U.S. Political Parties.* He is senior consulting editor on the Chelsea House series *Looking into the Past: People, Places, and Customs,* which examines past traditions, customs, and cultures of various nations.

Senior Consulting Editor ARTHUR M. SCHLESINGER, JR. is the preeminent American historian of our time. He won the Pulitzer Prize for his book *The Age of Jackson* (1945), and again for *A Thousand Days* (1965). This chronicle of the Kennedy Administration also won a National Book Award. He has written many other books, including a multi-volume series, *The Age of Roosevelt.* Professor Schlesinger is the Albert Schweitzer Professor of the Humanities at the City University of New York, and has been involved in several other Chelsea House projects, including the *American Statesmen* series of biographies on the most prominent figures of early American history.